W9-COJ-055

OPPORTUNITIES IN
SALES CAREERS

James Brescoll
Ralph M. Dahm

Revised by
Blythe Camenson

Foreword by
Bill Fox
Senior Vice President, Sales
Sony Corporation of America

VGM Career Books

Chicago   New York   San Francisco   Lisbon   London   Madrid   Mexico City
Milan   New Delhi   San Juan   Seoul   Singapore   Sydney   Toronto

331.7
B 842

Library of Congress Cataloging-in-Publication Data

Brescoll, James.
      Opportunities in sales careers / James Brescoll, Ralph M. Dahm; revised by Blythe
      Camenson; foreword by Bill Fox.
         p. cm.— (VGM opportunities series)
       ISBN 0-658-01646-6 (hardcover) ISBN 0-658-01647-4 (paperback)
       1. Selling—Vocational guidance I. Dahm, Ralph M., 1951–.   II. Title.   III. Series

   HF5438.25 .B733   2001
   658.85'023'73—dc21   2001026099

VGM Career Books

A Division of The **McGraw-Hill** *Companies*

Copyright © 2002 by The McGraw-Hill Companies. All rights reserved. Printed in the United States
of America. Except as permitted under the United States Copyright Act of 1976, no part of this
publication may be reproduced or distributed in any form or by any means, or stored in a database
or retrieval system, without the prior written permission of the publisher.

1 2 3 4 5 6 7 8 9 0 LBM/LBM 0 9 8 7 6 5 4 3 2 1

ISBN 0-658-01646-6 (hardcover)
ISBN 0-658-01647-4 (paperback)

This book was set in Times by Publication Services, Inc.
Printed and bound by Lake Book Manufacturing

Cover photograph copyright © PhotoDisc

McGraw-Hill books are available at special quantity discounts to use as premiums and sales
promotions, or for use in corporate training programs. For more information, please write to the
Director of Special Sales, Professional Publishing, McGraw-Hill, Two Penn Plaza, New York, NY
10121-2298. Or contact your local bookstore.

This book is printed on acid-free paper.

CONTENTS

ABOUT THE AUTHORS

James Brescoll has owned and operated a variety of small businesses—a specialty printing shop, public relations and advertising firms, and creative counseling and promotion agencies. To each he has committed his many talents of writing, photography (both still and video), art, printing, graphics design, layout, and conceptualization. He also increased productivity, performance, and profits.

His feature writing has appeared in more than 850 national, regional, and local publications; house organs; trade journals; daily and Sunday newspapers; and general-interest magazines. He continues to produce copy (with photographic and layout support) for advertising markets; business, professional, and social organizations; public relations agencies; and individuals. He has written and published two poetry/prose books, served as speechwriter for political candidates and corporate executives, and has been a practicing auctioneer. He provides consultation services to business firms in areas such as communications, motivation, employee development, and community relations.

Mr. Brescoll is a skilled professional photographer who holds varied photographic competition awards and honors. He is a dynamic and inspirational public speaker who addresses today's issues with insight and compassion.

His educational background includes a B.A. in photojournalism from San Jose State College, California, and completion of all requirements towards an M.A. degree in mass communications at San Jose State University.

He has been a feature writer and photo editor for Associated Press in New York City, an administrative assistant to a California state legislator, and a newspaper editor for a major auto manufacturing company and a leading national steel production firm.

Ralph M. Dahm began his sales career in the early 1970s as technical coordinator and then regional manager of international sales for Shure Brothers, Inc. He next became regional manager of international sales for Turner Division, CONRAC Corporation, in Cedar Rapids, Iowa.

He served as Midwest regional manager for Audio Technica, U.S., Inc., in Stowe, Ohio, and became division manager at Banner Personnel Service, Inc., Chicago. In 1982, Dahm & Associates, Inc. was established as a national recruiting firm specializing in marketing, sales, and technical positions and now operates as a management consultant firm.

In his sales positions, Dahm established and implemented product usage in sales promotions and seminars worldwide, initiated distribution programs throughout Far East nations, increased sales volume within a fourteen-state territory by 100 percent in one year, and raised overall division sales by 60 percent during a period of economic decline.

He has personally conducted hundreds of sales training seminars annually, ranked third among fifty-five employees for individual sales performance, was named company "Rep of the Year" two years in a row, and served as president of Sales & Marketing Executives of Chicago, 1985–1986.

Dahm has judged many Junior Achievement competitions and served as director of emergency room volunteers at Central DuPage Hospital in Winfield, Illinois.

Dahm established another corporation, D&D Distribution, Inc., in 1985. As president, he oversees a national sales network selling disposable medical products to hospitals, clinics, doctors' offices, and the Department of Veterans Affairs system of 175 hospitals and clinics. Additionally, D&D Distribution, Inc. has successfully completed twenty-three U.S. government supply contracts. The company specializes in selling products made in the United States, thereby promoting the growth of domestic corporations while assisting in the hiring and retaining of employees whose jobs are threatened by inexpensive products imported from other countries.

Dahm currently is creating another corporation to manufacture premium-quality latex examination gloves to be used primarily by paramedics and emergency medical services personnel. The company expects to produce three million gloves monthly and create more than forty new jobs in an economically depressed area in Illinois.

This edition has been thoroughly revised by Blythe Camenson. She was educated in Boston, earning her B.A. with a double major in psychology and English from the University of Massachusetts and her M.Ed. in counseling from Northeastern University. She worked in the mental health field for several years, then moved overseas and taught English as a foreign language in various universities in the Persian Gulf. Now based in Albuquerque, New Mexico, she is a full-time writer and director of Fiction Writer's Connection, a membership organization that helps new writers learn how to get published. Her website is at www.fictionwriters.com.

Blythe Camenson has more than four dozen books in print, most published by VGM Career Books. She is also the co-author of *Your Novel Proposal: From Creation to Contract* (Writer's Digest Books, 1999).

FOREWORD

"Sales," as defined by *Webster's Dictionary,* is "the transfer of title to property from one person to another for a price." All of us are involved in sales during our lives. It is a readily understood concept. The selling process, however, is not so simple. The "old school" concept of sales conjures up characters such as Willy Loman and Professor Harold Hill. Individuals who chose sales as a career were held in much the same esteem as we hold politicians today. A likable enough bunch of folks—just don't turn your back when you walk away. The farmer's daughter was to be kept under lock and key during the salesman's occasional visits.

Today, these stereotypes are all but forgotten. The modern sales professional is viewed as just that: a professional. As a career, sales offers an individual daily challenges and opportunities. Few careers offer as diverse a scope of tasks. A sales professional today is expected to be involved in all facets of the sale. In my business, the salesperson can act as product specialist, ad executive, merchandiser, expeditor, collector, and even shipper. All of these in one day, with one customer! Our sales personnel, as most, are expected to have a true entrepreneurial spirit. They must be capable of making sound decisions with an eye toward long-term impact. Additionally, today more than ever, each individual within an organization is held accountable for increasing the shareholder's value.

There is an almost infinite number of goods and services sold today. Sales professionals must possess certain qualities regardless of what they are selling. Sales is a "people business." Excellent communication skills are absolutely essential to a successful career in sales. Communication, by definition, is an active, two-way process. In sales, all facets of communication are vitally important. Obviously, you must be able to effectively communicate to prospective buyers as to why they should buy from you. It is equally important, though, to listen to customers in order to successfully interpret their specific needs. You must gain the trust and confidence of those buyers to make the sale. This ability to identify needs and overcome objections is what distinguishes a professional salesperson from a mere "order taker."

Organizational skills also are required. The sales professional must be sure that no detail slips through the cracks. Follow-up and follow-through skills are important elements of the sale. The proverbial "burnt bridge" can rarely be rebuilt today due to the fierce competitive nature of the sales business. Probably the most significant change in today's selling environment, since this text was originally published in the 1980s, is the competitive landscape. Today's competition cannot always be predicted. As the speed of technology has increased dramatically in recent years, more and more companies are broadening their focus. In the consumer electronics segment, for example, companies like Microsoft and AOL are vying for their own space in America's family rooms. They are introducing hardware products like televisions and game consoles showcasing their brand. As more traditional players in that realm, companies like mine now face competitors that we may not have anticipated only a few months before! Examples like this one exist in almost every sector. That's why selling your *brand* today is just as important as selling your goods or services. *Leverage* has become an essential strategic selling tool.

As with most other professions, in order to succeed in sales, you must set goals. An action plan to achieve these goals must be implemented. I have seen many people fail in our business due solely to their inability to plan. As I mentioned earlier, each sale is unique. It is relatively easy to become so totally consumed in the individual sale that the long-term goal is clouded. You must be sufficiently self-motivated to maintain your focus on those future goals. The true measure of a successful career in sales is gauged over the long-term.

Bill Fox
Senior Vice President, Sales
Sony Corporation of America

INTRODUCTION

To write one book about sales careers, where many books could encompass the many diverse sales areas, is both a challenge and an education. Within these pages you will find the career steps to follow, the actions to take, and the individual presentations you will need for personal success and financial reward.

It should be recognized that the sales profession is ever changing—growing with new challenges, concepts, and innovations that, often, are as complex as the ongoing developments within each area, whether they be manufacturing, service, or general industry.

For the individual, entering the sales field for a lifetime career is an important personal step. It is a decision that can lead to successful participation in the continued growth of our global economy. Whether one seeks an entry-level opportunity or a middle-management position, each sales level has its own challenges—from the largest manufacturer of specialized products to the smallest one-person operation.

In some sense, our world today runs not by government dictate but by sales effort; not by corporate success but by sales effort; not by increased technological growth in every area of social life but by sales effort; and not by decisive market trends but by sales effort.

The success of those who sell has opened the way for the ever increasing enrichment of many people. From the first recorded sales efforts through the complexities of today's modern world, salespeople have initiated the rise or fall of communities, states, and nations.

A major element in civilizations is the process of creation, manufacture, distribution, and sale of goods—a creation of buying markets and a source of income production upon which many social goals, values, and daily operations are based. Into this environment comes the salesperson skilled in the ways of commerce, personal psychology, finances, product knowledge, and consumer needs. He or she has goods that sustain the need for survival and, at the same time, give consumers choices—goods that can be used for entertainment, education, enlightenment, and enjoyment.

The modern salesperson is often a visionary; he or she sees what the future may hold by recognizing where the many products sold today can lead.

Salespeople are not born to be in sales. Their upbringing, environment, education, social attitudes, and personal traits all combine to make the forces that lead to becoming a salesperson. Although writers have portrayed the salesperson as a lonely and lost figure while out on the job, sales today requires much interaction between seller, management, company employees, customers, and the general public.

Sales is a job for those who recognize the need for professional guidance and understanding in a world where a "me first" attitude is too prevalent. It means having the integrity and self-discipline to do the assigned job in a manner that maintains a national forward movement and brings financial and personal success to the salesperson.

This book emphasizes the many sales areas open to the newcomer, but in the final analysis remember that all sales success is the product of, and results from, those who sell.

These pages highlight the necessary steps the individual can take to develop a successful sales career through personal development, education, professional experience, and determination.

The challenges within sales are many. The rewards can be tremendous. For those who seek such challenges and rewards, there is only one recommendation: Go for it!

CHAPTER 1

ARE YOU SALES ORIENTED?

"The secret of success is constancy to purpose."

Benjamin Disraeli
Earl of Beaconsfield
Speech (June 24, 1870)

Making a career choice is, for most people, one of the most difficult decisions of their lives. The majority of high-paying jobs require a college education. More specialized study, in turn, takes more education.

This investment of time and money should not be dictated by whim, chance, family pressures (often based on social expectations rather than practical knowledge or understanding), peer influences, or emulation of others' successes.

Since its earliest days, the sales arena has had to grow simply to stay ahead of the world's increasing population. Before any new territory was officially opened by governmental decree, salespeople had been among the first explorers, seeking new markets or expanding present markets, and in the process affecting future growth and determining the needs of those to follow—innovators and builders all.

1

To enter the sales arena today, a person must first recognize what benefits can be available through successful selling. More importantly, he or she should learn *before* entering sales what personal skills and attitudes will be necessary to make for the complete salesperson.

CHARACTERISTICS OF SALES

Even in today's highly technological society, there are unlimited sales opportunities for the newcomer. These range from "small-town selling" (dealing with a limited market with a limited number of customers) to "big-time selling" (finding, developing, and maintaining an extensive list of customers while selling any and all products needed by the customers). Regardless of where the individual ultimately settles within sales, there are certain basic characteristics shared by all successful sales careers.

Assigned Territories

This specialized sales area belongs to the salesperson alone, for no other salesperson within the firm can sell within this area. Sales territories are created based on such factors as population patterns, product use, the competition's position, and sales potential. It is up to the salesperson to enlarge the assigned territory through finding new accounts, while continuing to provide a greater-than-expected level of service to those customers already in hand.

Job Security

The average salesperson is seldom unemployed unless he or she has a serious personal handicap that drastically interferes with the selling job. Why?

In economic downturns, it is the salesperson who is expected to "keep the company ship afloat." The salesperson is called upon to find and sign accounts that create revenue, stimulate company business, and maintain productivity and employment. In good economic times, the salesperson is the hero, the one who makes it all happen with orders received. At the same time, more businesses in good times turn toward facility improvements, employee programs, and increased stocking of the most-needed items. This increases the salesperson's opportunities for more sales and an even higher success rate.

Salespeople today remain unique. They not only create a loyal customer following for their particular product but, in so doing, establish personal customer loyalty. Although today's customers have a much wider selection of goods and salespeople promoting those goods, it is the alert salesperson who emphasizes product loyalty above personal loyalty.

In earlier days, the drummer attitude of having the customer beholden to the salesperson worked because the salesperson was most often the only way goods could be delivered when and where needed. Today, quick transportation and easy communications have reduced this limitation within the sales process.

It would be a reckless or uncaring sales manager, however, who would fire a salesperson (regardless of cause) when the possibility exists that the individual could take perhaps twenty-five to thirty high-paying customers to a competitor.

Self-Supervision

The primary criterion a salesperson must meet can be summed up in one word: *results*. Though there is supervision from management, most salespeople are able to schedule their work habits in accordance with their own time frame. The basic idea, which works well, is to know what has to be done and do it. All other work-related tasks (such as paperwork, telephoning, correspondence, and order preparation and transmittal) can be done when more time is available, usually in the evening hours or during weekends.

Self-discipline is the primary requirement of self-supervision. It is the most difficult, yet most necessary, quality a salesperson must have. It overcomes an attitude of laxness toward the job that, in an office environment, would be totally unacceptable.

Without self-discipline—to make the next telephone call, visit the next customer, or file the necessary reports—no salesperson would long remain in sales with any hope for success.

Promotion

To receive a promotion requires that the salesperson demonstrate personal selling techniques on a daily basis. The seller's ability can be measured in the number of orders received, but it also is necessary to show certain qualities in dealing with co-workers.

The very techniques by which the salesperson succeeds with individual customers are those that enhance personal company growth. They include:

- ability to communicate effectively
- skill to get along with others
- concern toward the problems of others
- ability to solve buyer problems and overcome objections
- gift of consideration toward all
- recognition of positive attitudes in others
- avoidance of self-serving bragging in any way
- maintenance of commonsense attitudes in order to recognize all sides of issues
- positive mental attitudes

Recognition

Recognition is what makes salespeople tick! For good or bad, sales-people today gain recognition from all sides. Their work is studied by every company department and officer; it is, after all, from sales that company success or failure derives. The individual results of one salesperson's monthly sales sometimes can make or break company plans for years to come. These results also will reveal which sellers are not pulling their weight and so are on the way out.

Any successful salesperson's career is the result of long years of customer cultivation, product evaluation and study, and implementation of company policies and procedures. It is educational development and interpersonal relationship growth within the company. It is the potential for increased recognition and honors, enhanced by continual self-development. It is the individual acceptance of what has been done in the past and, more importantly, what has to be done in the future.

Self-Determination

Those who choose sales for a lifetime career may do so for many reasons. Some seek the image of the salesperson as a free spirit, the last frontier of self-determination; others see the job as a channel for personal commitment; still others see sales as a means of using individual skills to their best advantage.

Philip James Bailey highlighted this concept when he wrote in *A Country Town*:

> "He most lives who thinks most—feels the noblest—acts the best."

Through careful study, these people have found sales as a means to fill their need for success and challenge. They have taken time to carefully analyze their inner abilities, values, education, goals, personal needs and wants, background, and motivations, and have worked long and hard to develop their most positive qualities for purposes of a sales career. Such inner strength and determination are personal attitudes shared by other successful people across the industrial, manufacturing, and business world.

SKILLS AND QUALITIES YOU'LL NEED TO SUCCEED

Although it is desirable to possess the most positive traits within when contemplating a sales position, it is a sad truth that some individuals with everything going for them turn out to be life's never-rans, people who never worked to develop what skills they did have toward future goals and aspirations. Others, with seemingly less skill or fewer abilities, have risen to the top of their chosen careers through determination and personal development initiated and followed through by personal effort.

Every individual is different in terms of upbringing, attitude, goals, and interests. For salespeople of today, however, certain qualities must be present, and the more effortlessly they seem to come across, the better.

Personal Appearance

The first impression the salesperson creates comes when first meeting the customer. In that moment of confrontation, the buyer can react positively or negatively toward the individual's dress code (Is it appropriate for this meeting? Is it in keeping with this company's image? Can I feel confidence in this individual?); attitude (How does this person act? Can I recognize confidence in this salesperson's product because of this person? Does he or she reflect confidence and self-assurance?); and ability (Does this person know the product? Does this person know my company's goals and purpose? Can we receive what's ordered when specified and at an agreed-upon price? Will this person be there when needed in emergencies?).

The successful salesperson presents the best image possible and maintains that overall picture with every return visit—or until the buyer indicates more informal wear is justified.

Voice

The salesperson's voice, on the telephone or in person, can add a new dimension to the overall physical impression given. The sales voice should be well-modulated, warm, clearly spoken, interesting, and relaxing (though not to the point of creating boredom).

Like any successful public speaker, the skilled salesperson recognizes the unspoken time limit of the presentation. He or she must, therefore, be not only clear in sales preparation but concise in the vocal presentation. This leaves no room for the buyer's doubts about the individual or the product being promoted.

Listening

The most important aspect of sales success is the ability to listen well. Just as the salesperson will seek to incorporate all pertinent facts and information into the sales presentation, so he or she should learn early to listen—to really hear all the facts and pertinent information provided by the buyer—because this is vital to bringing about the successful closing of the sale.

It is necessary to allow for time when the salesperson can concentrate on what is really being said. This "time of silence" allows the assimilation of critical information—the buyer's company plans and future needs, personal interests, and outside activities—which is material to be drawn from in subsequent meetings to increase informality and customer confidence in the salesperson. Also, a realistic appraisal from today's medical research indicates that people are most activated and enthused when talking about, or listening to others talk about, themselves.

For the salesperson, to develop listening skills really means to listen—to set aside inner mental ramblings and observations to concentrate totally on what the buyer is saying and doing. The good listener possesses a powerful sales tool.

Poise

Selling, at its easiest, is only a matter of properly filling an order blank for a motivated buyer and submitting that paperwork to the company. At its most difficult, the salesperson must draw upon every skill, all knowledge, and innovative sales techniques developed on the spot to reach a disgruntled or indifferent buyer. An ability to overcome negative buyer attitudes shows poise (easy, self-possessed assurance of manner) and acts to maintain the seller's presentation while offering the buyer new product information necessary to fulfill the buyer's needs.

Dependability

The major success any salesperson can claim toward a customer is "the buyer knows I can be counted on." Such confidence is the cornerstone of securing the customer's continued business. If the buyer feels certain that products ordered will arrive when scheduled at the agreed-upon price, then that salesperson has done an effective job of displaying personal commitment to the customer.

He or she has, for the most part, accepted one cardinal rule of life:

> "This above all—to thine own self be true, And it must follow as the night the day thou canst not be false to any man."
>
> —William Shakespeare
> *Hamlet 1:3*

Of course, there will be times when something goes wrong. A damaged, delayed, or poorly wrapped shipment can happen. When it does, the professional salesperson will, upon hearing of the problem, determine the cause, initiate immediate steps to solve the problem (to customer satisfaction), and then follow the matter to conclusion. This instant-action approach reassures the customer that her or his interests remain the number-one priority of both salesperson and company.

Enthusiasm

To sell successfully, the salesperson must have what Norman Vincent Peale calls "the priceless quality that makes everything different—enthusiasm." He or she must know and believe in the product. To have a buyer purchase those products and/or services, the salesperson also must reflect a personal enthusiasm in the product and/or service and its ability to fill customer needs. The more enthusiastic the salesperson, the more quickly the buyer will be caught up in that positive feeling and sign on the dotted line. Such feelings, however, must be genuine or the buyer will recognize sales apathy and look elsewhere for satisfaction.

Self-Confidence and Self-Esteem

There is one major difference between self-esteem and self-confidence: self-confidence comes from product knowledge and the understanding of how that product can fulfill the buyer's needs; self-esteem comes from an inner sense of pride, enthusiasm, interest, and involvement with the product and the buyer. It is self-esteem that forms the image of success that others see.

Education

No salesperson, no matter how learned, and whether presently enrolled for learning or not, can ever have enough education.

Aristotle said, when asked how much educated men were superior to the uneducated; "as much as the living are to the dead."

The opportunity to attend seminars, workshops, and educational programs (whether college-based or industry-formed) is an ongoing part of every salesperson's continuous education. Studies in general education courses (for example, communications, sales fundamentals, English, psychology, speaking, and advertising) could take a decade or more. Yet each learning opportunity only increases the salesperson's effectiveness and success. Beyond these basics, which the salesperson recognizes as vital to success, are additional opportunities. For those seeking to enrich job duties with more knowledge and activities, the horizons are unlimited.

"Know thyself" refers not only to facts and figures about one's life, but to the daily knowledge and philosophy formed through a sharing of ideas, dreams, goals, and business, and through drawing on personal information that provides continual new insights into individuals encountered daily. After all:

> "Nothing that was worthy in the past departs; no truth or goodness realized by man ever dies; or can die."
>
> —Thomas Carlyle
> *Sir Walter Scott* (1838)

In seriously considering a sales career, the fledgling salesperson can and must initiate inner growth and personal development so that, in years to come, individual customers will say, "That person is more than a mere representative of the company and product line. He or she takes a personal involvement in our operations and our people, for both the good and bad times. He or she is totally dependable and our company is better for having had this contact."

Obtaining such a compliment comes only through personal development and growth within the salesperson's carefully planned career.

Personality

The combination of a person's individual qualities, including mental, social, religious, ethical, business, and moral values, makes up the trait we call "personality."

Together with appearance and attitude, these qualities become one's personality, as shaped by the everyday world and many inner and outer factors. Because the formation of an individual takes place every day, it can be successfully adapted toward a positive sales career through certain steps:

- continual self-improvement
- self-determination toward inner growth
- personal evaluation by self-analysis as to one's assets and liabilities; evaluation by others; a blending of self-evaluation with the insights of others toward personal development goals
- developing an outgoing personality
- adopting an aggressive but not offensive style

Good Judgment

It takes good judgment and common sense to make sales opportunities work. More than guesswork, good judgment involves knowing when and how to make the right decision regarding customer needs.

As a salesperson gains in practical knowledge through training and on-the-job experience, he or she also learns the methods by which to prepare presentations to fit the customer's time, needs, and attitudes. Such a presentation includes highlights of the product, necessary product information and materials, prices, warranties, discounts, special features, and pertinent details linked to customer usage. An indication of informed judgment by the salesperson is that the presentation earns customer attention, respect, and trust. A good presentation will enable a buyer to make an informed decision; it will overcome the objections prior to their being verbalized.

Alertness

To sell successfully requires thinking at all times—planning, observing, relating, incorporating, and learning and reacting on a moment-to-moment basis. The alert salesperson is constantly "tuned in" to recognize opportunities and problems equally and to adapt quickly, so that he or she can handle both favorably. He or she is aware at all times of the infinite nuances of customer goals and plans and is able to provide the necessary support to fulfill buyer planning.

Being alert entails knowing, at a glance, how to judge a person through clothing, attitude, voice, and message—then openly and honestly dealing effectively with that person.

Imagination

A popular motivational quote, authored by Napolean Hill, says:

"What the mind of man can conceive and believe, the mind of man can achieve."

—Think and Grow Rich

That is the end result of imagination. When the salesperson draws upon experiences, good and bad, to formulate effective new selling procedures—that's imagination. When the salesperson develops product innovations providing the customer with new means of productivity and personnel utilization—that's imagination. When the salesperson recognizes new means and methods for product distribution, use, and recycling that enhance customer growth—that's imagination.

Imagination is creativity on the loose. It improves customer relations, stimulates real product growth, provides enhanced opportunities throughout the marketing area, and gives the customer the inner satisfaction of knowing there is strong imaginative support available from the salesperson and her or his company.

Memory

The salesperson who remembers names, special days, personal habits, and the business styles of customers has a strong support tool in the work kit.

Memory doesn't happen automatically. As the individual ages, memory cells within the brain die by the billions daily. Little, yet vital, facts are suddenly lost when most needed. But memory is, like most selling skills, a result of personal development and hard work. Simply put, memory skills can be improved and sustained through particular practices and programs available in books and through educational training courses.

The salesperson who recognizes the benefits of a well-developed memory works each day to maintain performance in memory. Thus, when returning to a particularly valued customer a third or fourth time, the effective salesperson is able to make references to that individual's family or golf habits as part of the conversation (not suddenly uttered to impress but simply mentioned as a natural part of the conversation).

There are no easy steps to improve or enhance memory skills. Through steady work and continual concentration using materials available, an individual can improve memory and increase his or her job performance.

Showmanship

The successful salesperson knows showmanship—the means of presenting the product or service beyond a prepared sales text.

This skill requires more than using one-liner jokes, back-slapping camaraderie, or gimmicks. It is positive use of innovative sales steps, which seeks to:

1. *Fulfill expectations.* The buyer expects certain action from the salesperson: honesty, expertise, ethics, courtesy, knowledge, commitment, and a quality product/service. The salesperson who fails to fulfill such expectations through daily actions does not fulfill his or her responsibilities to company or buyer.
2. *Enjoy the relationship.* The salesperson lets the buyer know, by word and performance, the business relationship is something special and highly valued.
3. *Inspire confidence.* The salesperson openly discusses her or his firm's product/service and its value to the buyer's operation through effective use of product/service information, knowledge of the buyer's needs, and a detailed projection of seller/buyer relations over the future. This allows the buyer to know she or he is served by a supportive and enriching salesperson.
4. *Sell "self."* Selling the product/service, for the salesperson, is often easier, but far less productive, than selling "self." The salesperson able to sell "self" before product/service forms a stronger foundation with the buyer that allows the promotion and sale of products needed by the buyer. Such "self" sale assures the buyer that the seller will work toward a long-term beneficial relationship to serve both well.

HOW TO INVENTORY SKILLS AND INTERESTS FOR SALES WORK

If selling is the career you seek, ask yourself several important questions to determine your immediate inner reactions to the selling process. Such questions should include:

1. Do I really enjoy meeting new people?
2. Do I really want or need to help others?
3. Do I function better dealing with people or working with objects?
4. Am I sensitive to others' feelings?
5. Is my thinking practical, ordered, and arranged?
6. Can I function effectively under long hours and in stressful conditions?
7. Are other people to be manipulated or to be dealt with openly and honestly at all times?
8. Will my family (now or proposed) accept my position and travel commitments and responsibilities?
9. Am I emotionally mature enough to handle the sharing and problems of a selling position?
10. Am I willing to commit myself to the requirements of the job?

There are many people who are incapable of becoming a salesperson at any level. They are uncomfortable trying to "sell" others, unsure of themselves, uninterested in taking the risks of selling, and unwilling to believe totally in any product or service.

If, however, a person feels sales oriented and has the personality, potential, and confidence to successfully find, apply for, and obtain a selling job, then certain qualities must be immediately weighed.

Understanding

The salesperson must recognize the customer's position relative to the product and its applications to customer operations. This insight allows the planning, development, and presentation of the product line to be more closely attuned to customer anticipations and needs.

While providing as much information as possible to assist the customer's choice, the knowledgeable salesperson also develops a concentrated strategy for learning about the future goals and opportunities that will arise within a customer's company.

Mutual Communications

When two minds are thinking alike, the results often can be overwhelming. The salesperson who shares the customer's visions and knows how to incorporate the products available into such visions will be much more successful than one who simply fills order forms without looking ahead. The customer, recognizing a kindred soul in the salesperson, will become more open and expansive, thus providing opportunities that might otherwise have been passed up.

Belief

Unless a salesperson believes in the product being sold and in the customer's need for such a product, a communications bond will not be established. The customer often will not find it possible to believe either in the product or the salesperson. By letting the customer share in the inner feelings and insights, the salesperson establishes a more productive relationship.

Action

The final step in effectively dealing with the customer lies in the salesperson's response in closing the sale through a personal call to action. Whether it is to obtain a signed order or a commitment for future orders, the salesperson must move the customer to positive action and maintain that attitude throughout the relationship.

Maintaining a Good Record

Potential salespeople, though satisfied they hold the necessary qualities for selling, find potential employers asking for more detailed information. Besides the standard resume information—name, address, telephone number, employment objective, past employment record and history, educational background, special skills, languages spoken, honors and awards, personal data, and related experiences—there are personnel forms that ask for details of health, estimate of future potential (based on company-sponsored tests and interviews), earning ability as a salesperson, personal evaluations, job performance reviews, and other pertinent information considered necessary to better understand the individual. This material remains with a salesperson throughout her or his career. It acts as a corporate road map of personal success or failure, of growth and accomplishment. Most important, it is a record of individual adherence to the basic principles of successful salesmanship.

CHAPTER 2

SALES IN REVIEW

"Men of genius do not excel in any profession because they
labour in it; but they labour in it because they excel."

William Hazlitt
Characteristics

Selling today is a major influence in all areas of an individual's life.
It identifies needs and promotes ever increasing development and
distribution of goods while, most importantly, creating demand.
Selling expands into the nonmaterial world of dreams, emotions,
ideas, and the idle speculations of the creative mind.

Its purpose is defined as:

> *sales*—of, relating to, or used in selling.
>
> *sell*—to give up (property) to another for something of
> value (as money); to offer for sale; to give up in return for
> something else. . . .
> *Merriam Webster's Collegiate Dictionary*

SALES OBJECTIVES

Some form of selling exists wherever the human mind and human commerce exist—if not to "give up (property)" then to provide evidence that supports the buyer's personal needs and views.

Such selling has always been done efficiently (doing something well) and effectively (producing a desired result) and exists in every product advertisement and commercial viewed by a potential buyer, as well as in word-of-mouth discussions on the pros and cons of various products. Every product creates the power of selling simply by its existence.

Selling, in today's marketplace, can be:

- *Positive*—"This product can really make your life easier!"
- *Negative*—"Support an end to animal research!"
- *Personal*—one-on-one in small groups
- *Impersonal*—a massive promotional and advertising effort without human involvement or relationship
- *Immediate*—"Buy now and receive in return . . ."
- *Long-term*—"You've known this product for years . . ."
- *One-issue*—"Save the spotted Australian Outback salamander!"
- *Neutral*—"Buy United States Bonds today."

Selling is broken down into four primary areas of action:

1. *Retail:* The buyer comes to the seller in search of specific products.
2. *Wholesale:* The seller goes to the buyers (usually store buyers or purchasing agents) at specified times to promote a specific product line or group of products.
3. *Specialties:* Usually a sales presentation is needed for such items as real estate, office equipment, insurance, or securities—once the buyer is reached.

4. *Door-to-door:* The seller has all the information or products for immediate inspection, demonstration, and questions. The most difficult part of this selling form is "getting in the door," which is often said to be 50 percent of the sale itself.

Selling, through dedicated and professional salespeople, now goes far beyond the requirements of the order book. Salespeople today must know their products and services thoroughly—not only to maintain, but to increase the role of sales within the total global economy.

Though salespeople prosper primarily based on their individual performance, the salesperson's career is usually economically rewarding, socially expanding, and personally fulfilling.

If all forms of selling were suddenly removed from the world, our civilization's complex social structure would quickly disintegrate.

A BRIEF HISTORY OF SALES

From America's earliest days, when salespersons initiated the movement of goods to all compass points, selling has been in constant change. It has evolved into a primary and integral part of national life and has made innumerable contributions to the lifestyle and wellbeing of people everywhere.

The work of sales and selling has changed dramatically since taking root within the earliest societies. Then, as now, those who sold were responsible for many human advances.

Selling was an active industry as far back as 2500 B.C., when traveling salespeople moved across vast deserts with market caravans and over wide water, transporting goods and ideas to all corners of the known world. By the time Christopher Columbus opened a water route to America, salespeople were already the unseen movers and shakers of civilized society.

By the early 1880s in America, salespeople (known more commonly as "drummers," "Yankee peddlers," or "commercial travelers") had succeeded in creating an overall image of themselves as the "free and easy" type—willing to swap stories, smile a lot, slap backs, and muss little children's hair as adoring mothers looked on. Such efforts, however, more often tended to sell the individual than the product.

This personal effort, which swept across America with every new exploration and discovery, laid down a strong and ever expanding foundation for transforming the seller within a "seller's market" (demand exceeds supply) to one working within a "buyer's market" (supply exceeds demand).

In the westward drive of settlers across America, sellers made sure the goods and materials needed for everyday life were brought to the proper destinations from eastern United States markets. In this extended period of growth and expansion, the entrepreneur rose to develop and maintain the steady flow of goods and services to those markets initially found and developed by sellers.

It was, however, salespeople who started the cycle of productivity. Newfound markets sparked a need to fill those markets, which triggered individual creativity to provide goods and services for these new markets and in turn generated new production facilities and innovations. This increased the number of salespeople moving outward seeking new and larger markets, fostering a need for further expansion and leading to the growth and the creation of a whole new set of duties and responsibilities for salespeople.

SALES: DUTIES AND RESPONSIBILITIES

The services the seller provides extend beyond the technical advice and the information available. A partnership exists between seller and buyer in which, in a diverse market where the variety of product availability can be overwhelming, the seller is turned to as the source of product knowledge and dependability.

Selling is, at its core, a direct-communications effort aimed at satisfying the individual's particular needs regarding style, price, quality, durability, reputation, and dependability. Selling attempts to favorably sway a person's thought processes toward the product being sold as a means of fulfilling these needs.

Though effective sellers can change the reluctant buyer's mind, it is recognized that the buyer's personal buying habits are formed from social expectations, previous product usage, and ingrained bias. To overcome this type of buyer mind-set requires that the seller use a wide range of socially beneficial practices and goals in a total service concept.

This concept goes beyond the standard seller/buyer roles to involve both in a more personal relationship through continuous seller commitment. This requires a salesperson who *cares* about his or her firm's product, presentation, and follow-up, and extends this commitment to all aspects of the buyer's business, needs, personal feelings and reactions, and everyday activities.

Moreover, total service emphasizes the seller's willingness to discuss questions raised by the buyer in an honest and tactful manner; his or her dedication to relating the product to buyer productivity; and a guarantee that all complaints will be resolved to the buyer's satisfaction.

Total service is, for the salesperson, "being there" at every opportunity to support, advise, instruct, and motivate the buyer through positive use of her or his personality, patience, persuasion, perseverance, and product promotion—the end result being a harmonious relationship that the buyer appreciates, remembers, shares with other potential buyers, and turns to in times of company need.

To the salesperson, total service means incorporating the following actions into buyer relationships on a daily basis.

Fulfilling Personal Needs

Effective selling can quickly show a customer what is available to enhance or improve a personal lifestyle, where the product can be obtained, and at what price. Knowledgeable salespeople at the product outlet provide information adding to the buyer's understanding, while highlighting the benefits of the product.

Encouraging Better Products

By continually exploring buyer interest, the seller can formulate new product lines to better aid buyer goals. At the same time, the seller may find applications for current products in another area. (Many products originally designed for specific markets have been modified and developed to meet general consumer use.)

Expanding Product Markets

Because buyers are becoming increasingly more selective in personal product choice and use, new products have found demand within all consumer levels. This demand has required that sellers expand their individual sales efforts.

Developing Knowledgeable Consumers

Through effective and creative selling methods, today's sellers, whether working within a company setting or acting as independent agents, are able to highlight the necessity and value of their products, provide new insights and understanding of goods and services, and help the buyer recognize needs and goals. The seller understands the buyer's desire to solve an immediate problem as quickly as possible (for the lowest cost and best quality), and that the buyer may turn to the seller for guidance and aid. The buyer looks to the seller for information on competing products in order to form a satisfactory and sensible buying decision.

Maintaining the Free Market

The seller of goods, services, or ideas helps maintain the continuity of free market development and growth. Through advertising, promotion, door-to-door campaigns, direct mailings, telephone solicitation, and personal commitment, the seller gives the buyer alternatives in product choice. Such activity increases competition and, in so doing, raises material quality and product availability.

Seller-to-Customer Communications

To successfully ply the trade, the seller must initiate dialogue between seller and buyer. Such effort is perceived as personal interest in the buyer's needs and dreams and will succeed where indifference or simple order-filling fails. Simply stated, the seller must *like* the buyer, as well as take a true interest in understanding the buyer's attitudes and purposes. This understanding, which easily initiates the sharing of ideas (namely, future product-planning goals from the seller and dreams and needs from the buyer) also means an ever increased attitude of goodwill toward the seller's goods and services. Such a one-on-one attitude recognizes a mutual "working together" philosophy held by both seller and buyer, a sharing of two or more minds toward a recognized end—the successful sale of seller products to the satisfaction of the buyer.

The Art of Persuasion

The successful salesperson learns early that buyers cannot be forced to purchase any product they do not want. Instead, a salesperson will utilize all means of product information at hand, developing and using imaginative methods of persuasion directed toward the buyer's acceptance of a specific product for personal benefit and use. At the same time, the seller seeks to bring the buyer into the sales effort through personal commitment (for example, seeking buyer input on product warranties, payment plans, improvements, and other suggestions).

SALES OPPORTUNITIES AHEAD

The result of successful American sales programs is easily recognized: This nation is the best-housed, best-traveled, best-clothed, best-educated, best-entertained, and best-fed of all the world's nations—and this applies to the majority of the American population rather than to just a privileged few.

There are two primary types of sellers today: those who sell to commercial, manufacturing, industrial, and retail firms and who remain almost totally unknown to the everyday consumer; and the salespersons employed within the walls of the millions of large and small businesses who sell directly to the consumer, such as retail outlets.

Other sellers, namely door-to-door solicitors and specialty marketers (those who sell such products as gold and silver or stock investments), are slowly being replaced by the mass-marketing, direct-mail, telemarketing, and television services maintained through computer technology at reasonable costs.

Each type of salesperson draws from a wide knowledge of the psychological, physiological, social, and emotional forces influencing individual buying decisions. Marketing and advertising methods that use computers and other high-tech equipment have created accurate buyer/user assessments and analysis only speculated upon in earlier years. Sales technologies have been refined through in-depth research and testing within institutional responses, while subliminal perceptions and reactions are matched with interpersonal relationships in order to achieve market impact and buyer response.

Specialists trained in one field (for example, engineering or finance) now create their individualized selling programs for general buyer use. In doing so, they not only establish their leadership in a newly developed area of expertise, but challenge others in related areas to expand their knowledge in a "catch-up-and-keep-up" philosophy.

More and more opportunities are becoming available in the selling fields. Many firms, recognizing the vital necessity for an efficient and effective sales force, now provide additional employee training, education, and on-the-job experiences directed toward generating higher participation and productivity.

Schools that once carried a few sales and sales-related courses affiliated with other educational areas now offer basic and advanced courses in sales, sales management, and sales techniques.

Private companies, whether large or small, are sponsoring such education-related sales programs as Junior Achievement. In Junior Achievement, high school students create their own company, produce a viable product, and sell that product using all sales techniques available. There are also seminars, workshops, sales training courses, and personalized educational sessions instructing sales personnel in both the latest and the time-tested methods for success.

THE SELLER AND THE CUSTOMER: PERSONAL VIEWS

Today, the successful seller acts as a guide to help buyers select which product, of the many available, is best for their needs.

Such a role within society takes diverse forms yet is vital to seller (and the production facility represented), buyer (for the availability of new products and services), and the many others involved in the unending flow of materials each day.

The seller, whether on the road with order book in hand or standing behind a store counter, is the first and often the only link connecting the buyer with company products, philosophy, and potential. The seller, in today's world, is expected to sell not only the products of interest to the buyer but all other products offered by her or his company, of which the buyer may have no knowledge. The successful seller must know, then, not only the firm's products, output, quality, prices, availability, and guarantees but also the needs, future growth plans, management decisions, labor or union influences, and development and application of competitors' products.

These constantly changing facts and figures must daily be aligned with personal study of the international, national, regional, state, county, and local governmental rules and regulations that affect the products and the profession.

THE SALES ROLE IN BUSINESS

In fulfilling such broad-based requirements in the course of doing the job, today's seller has become a true professional in many areas beyond simply selling.

Product Advisor

Through daily communication with customers, the seller learns about problems associated with individual products. This knowledge is relayed to the engineering and production specialists of the firm in the form of seller input regarding modifications, recommendations, and improvements based on customer comments.

Service

Besides being able to provide knowledgeable advice and suggestions on products sold, the seller has the additional responsibility of providing customers with thoughtful answers and background information supported by company-backed actions and materials that educate and enlighten. Based on such available data, the unsure or hesitant buyer learns better how to select the proper materials, service, or equipment, and whether the product or service will accomplish corporate or personal goals. This relationship between the seller and the buyer provides for ongoing growth beneficial for both sides.

Public Relations

Today's seller must know not only how personally to sell the product but how to promote that product for maximum impact. This requires an understanding of pricing, promotion, and publicity programs and strategies. It is critical that the seller be able to project buyer acceptance in order to determine accurate sales figures upon which to base all public relations efforts.

Finances

The seller must know not only her or his firm's product line and prices but also the prices and benefits offered by the competition. At the same time, the seller must be attuned to the financial status of every buyer and compile the detailed information upon which a working sales program can be developed to fit the needs and finances of the buyer.

Communications

Though early salespeople only had to take orders, submit them, and follow through to delivery, the salesperson today must prepare many types of communications for management: detailed reports, guidelines, recommendations, product improvements, personnel reviews, analyses, customer promotional and marketing efforts, business correspondence, and less-formal daily feedback. Such feedback, dealing with buyer attitudes, insights, complaints, compliments, and suggestions regarding both the products and company policies, often is the company's first and only input from those toward whom their products or services are directed. This requires the salesperson to be a skilled communicator in dealing with all company areas relating to product, promotion, and management decisions.

PERSONAL REWARDS

For his or her efforts as a multifaceted company representative, the salesperson will receive, for education and job enhancement, the accumulated knowledge and experience of the firm's own public relations team, advertising and promotion services, product testing and quality research, engineering studies, marketing and planning papers, technical recommendations, and management decisions and directions.

In performing successfully, the salesperson is a "jack of all trades and a master of most." The knowledge involved develops and expands from the seller's personal efforts, educational opportunities, and more comprehensive and specialized company-sponsored training seminars and workshops. The successful seller also knows the effectiveness of intelligently and sensitively applying all this knowledge toward each customer's specific needs.

Today's sales representative is, thus, a skilled innovator—a problem recognizer who quickly becomes a problem solver, for her or his own daily success and that of the customers.

Men and women who have developed these qualities have learned the key ingredient to successful selling: the ability to persuade others toward a preselected choice of action, product, or idea.

Persuasion is the salesperson's strongest and most frequently practiced tool. Its use recognizes a mutual and collaborative relationship between seller and buyer, a sharing of two or more minds with an acknowledged goal in sight—the closing of a successful sale to the mutual satisfaction of both parties.

With persuasion the buyer recognizes in the salesperson's efforts the way that benefits are obtained and the possibilities of individual choice. Without persuasion and the attitude of self-confidence and belief it creates, no amount of goodwill, knowledge, enthusiasm, or commitment on the part of the sales representative would be enough to produce completed sales.

More and more men and women enter the workforce in the sales area. Whether for a large or small firm, as a "rep" for many firms, or simply to sell their "self" and an unknown product or dream with large potential, they are carrying on the old "drummer" tradition.

These individuals have worked and studied long hours to develop the basic sales skills upon which their life's work will move forward. They tenaciously apply the basic tenets of selling: learning the product; studying the potential buyer; communicating with the buyer in order to present the product; having up-to-date information available for buyer reference; and achieving the goal of the whole process—the sale.

It takes special attitudes and outlooks to become a successful salesperson. In the words of St. Francis of Assisi: "Start by doing what is necessary, then what is possible, and suddenly you are doing the impossible." To the searching and committed practitioner, the results can be the highest rewards available.

CHAPTER 3

SELLING THE PRODUCT

"He who would distinguish the true from the false must
have an adequate idea of what is true and false."

Benedict (Baruch) Spinoza
Ethics

The first decision you, as a fledgling salesperson, must make is what
you want to sell—tangibles (products that can be seen, felt, used
physically) or intangibles (products that are actions, promises, or
guarantees of service). A tangible product is usually easier to sell
than an intangible service. The customer can look, prod, weigh, test,
and then decide. Selling an intangible is harder, for the sales representative must be able to verbalize the benefits available to the buyer.

Selling, either tangible or intangible, is a complex interrelation
of the product (manufacturer and distribution) moving within varied outlets (retail, wholesale, specialty) to reach the final customer
(the individual consumer).

THE BASIC TYPES OF SALES POSITIONS

Up to this point, we have discussed seller-buyer relationships from
the manufacturing sales viewpoint—the selling of a product in
exclusive territories by company salespeople to selective specialized

33

buyers. For the person who considers sales, however, there is a wide variety of sales positions available.

Manufacturer Sales

In manufacturer sales, salespeople work directly to sell manufactured consumer or industrial goods to purchasing agents or company buyers in factories, hospitals, major retail stores, distributors, government and other public agencies, and schools—locations that require the specific products for further manufacture, for necessary supplies, for resale, or as equipment, production, operation, or service support.

These sales representatives may be assigned large territories that require heavy travel and extensive product knowledge for effectively dealing with buyer expectations. Such buyers, usually experienced individuals who know their market thoroughly, also recognize what the competition is doing to develop the market and cannot be fooled, high-pressured, or pleaded with for a sale. Manufacturer sales is a wide-open field, seen in terms of personal sales development.

Wholesaler Sales

The primary role of the wholesaler salesperson is to sell and stock products to retail and industrial outlets. Such sales are not made to the final customer but rather are sold to a middleman, who in turn has salespeople selling to the ultimate consumer.

Geographically, the wholesaler territory is considerably smaller than that of the manufacturer's sales representative, but there are many customers in the smaller area, and each is carefully developed in a harmonious relationship with the seller.

Wholesaling brings manufactured goods of all types together for overall distribution to retailers and industrial users. The salesperson provides continuous updating of the thousands of products available to the market, demonstrates particular products of interest to buyers, and maintains a continual buyer-feedback program to manufacturers.

Retail Sales

Retailing is the final step for the majority of products manufactured and distributed today. Communities have many large and small retail stores that the consumer can patronize. Products are available in all sizes, shapes, weights, and purposes, though many retail stores prefer specialization in particular products. The retail salesperson can find the greatest opportunity to enhance personal selling skills and sales presentations. In dealing with customers' specific product needs, this salesperson also learns about the particular products sold, as well as about the daily operations that include stocking, inventory, management practices, supervision, and meeting with wholesaler representatives to determine needed purchases. The opportunities for learning and advancement to more serious responsibilities is greater within the retail sales area, though the financial rewards are not as great as those of other sales areas.

A major benefit of retail selling is the opportunity for educational training through workshops, seminars, and in-house programs directed toward enhanced selling techniques and customer relationships.

Detail Sales

This is usually an entry-level position with a producer of consumer packaged goods (that is, health and beauty aids or other personal products). A major responsibility as a detail salesperson is to be a merchandise consultant to the retailer—to promote sales through creating goodwill with available customers. Detail sales representatives are most useful in promoting new products in support of already established retailers. They make sure the products are displayed in the most attractive fashion and often conduct in-store demonstrations or provide customers with small samples of new products. Before the detail salesperson goes "on the road," he or she receives thorough training in the latest product use and application. This, in turn, is passed on to customers through the best sales methods and materials available for promotion and sale of the product.

The detail salesperson, because he or she is *not* an order taker, can dedicate the total presentation and follow-up time to providing information, administration, availability, results, and future product associations for the customer. Such conduct requires great practice in tact, friendliness, sincerity, honesty, and an ethical standard that successfully represents the parent company.

Home Sales

Another taxing sales position is door-to-door sales. The salesperson arrives with product in hand, offering low cost, immediate benefit to the customer, and adaptability to the home or business environment visited.

Door-to-door selling success is based on volume and requires the sales representative to canvass large residential or business sections daily, be persuasive enough to get in the door, and then successfully sell as quickly as possible. Some roadblocks to accomplishment include:

- prospect not at home
- prospect not interested
- prospect unwilling or too uneasy to communicate
- prospect too busy to listen to presentation
- aggressive animals outside the selected premises
- posted "no soliciting allowed" signs
- local ordinances or neighborhood regulations

Good salespersons will not let the above objections deter them. They will find it a challenge, new and different each day. To compensate for the negative reaction to home salespeople, proffered sales commissions are usually higher per unit than other sales reps' commissions (26 percent of the product's sales price is not unusual).

Consumer Service Sales

This sales position deals in particular service and information of detailed products as needed by customers. Such services can range from insurance needs of all kinds through real estate activities and financial investment programs. To sell effectively under the consumer service requirements means the salesperson must be highly knowledgeable within the particular field involved (including knowing all laws at all levels, local to national trends, activities, and legal ramifications), so as to provide continual updating of information needed by the buyers. This salesperson must obtain all licenses required in the particular field.

Route Sales

The route salesperson has varied responsibilities to the customers receiving specific goods. This seller may serve dairies, bakeries, laundries and dry cleaners, or vending routes. They deliver ordered goods on a timely basis, respond to customer concerns or complaints, seek new market opportunities, and enhance customer satisfaction as needed.

When required, the route salesperson will process transactions for delivered goods and, at the same time, maintain detailed records of cash intake and outgo in an up-to-date fashion. Route sellers also are responsible for ensuring delivery of the product. They receive both salary and a percentage of sales made as financial compensation.

Specialty Sales

At one extreme, specialty goods can be expensive, intermittently purchased, and long lasting. At the other, specialty selling involves the recipient's purchasing varied items for household or personal needs from specialty stores (linen, televisions, or appliances).

The specialty salesperson has a broad-based market: individual customers and consumers at factories, special services (hospitals, school, libraries), shopping centers, and other locales. Here the sales representative deals in high-priced quality goods or high-quantity products.

In some instances, specialty sales work does not pay commissions as in other sales areas. However, determining between a salary or commission will be based on products, sales amount, turnover, and expenses involved.

Like other salespeople, the specialty salesperson must know how properly to sell the products available. For the higher-priced items, this requires technical understanding of the product gained through company training or through available educational courses. In the case of some specialty products (insurance, encyclopedia sets, home improvement products), the sellers often set up evening appointments at the potential customer's home, allowing for both husband and wife to be given a full presentation. This sales effort can take several hours and allows a total review of the product, financial commitment and terms, and specialty information available.

Though not all service salespersons are as inactive as the Maytag repairman featured on television commercials, a well-qualified service sales representative providing needed services recognizes that product turnover is minimal. This is why such a salesperson, to earn a good wage within his or her area of expertise, will work to find new customers while expanding the present sales to customers already being serviced.

THE INTERNET

This communications system demands highly educated and product-skilled salespeople—people to make initial contacts, provide arrangements, oversee production and distribution, coordinate promotional and public relations efforts, fulfill sales needs and goals, and enhance the personal touch through daily customer contact. Such activities, delivered through personal contact and associative outlets, will ensure a steady cash flow from which business and industry will finance the continual upgrading of this "information superhighway."

TELEVISION

Easy television (and telephone) access allows the salesperson to reach more than one customer when necessary. Conference calling (linking of many individuals or groups into one communications system) and videotaped sales presentations are but two readily available and very effectively used technology sales areas.

A more immediate development within the sales field that seriously concerns many retail outlets is television's effective reach into America's millions of homes (most with at least one TV set and countless millions with personal computers) that could serve as a mass-marketing outlet. In recent years, these varied network efforts have evolved into several very different sales areas.

Home Shopping

Home shopping, via television, was initiated by Home Shopping Network, Inc., in the late 1970s and QVC Network, Inc., in 1986. This service today continues to offer all firms marketing a product or service a large consumer audience for a low-cost distribution system. The home shopping operations, unlike retail competition, do *not* need thousands of stores nationwide or thousands of pieces of inventory at each store. The retailer's major in-store expenses—rent, sales personnel, and advertising—are dramatically reduced within the home shopping services, which are designed to sell goods directly to customers through on-camera product demonstrations via cable or broadcast television. Manufacturing representatives and salespeople also sell these promoted goods within their specific sales field while working to find and fulfill further sales opportunities.

Home Shopping Network, Inc., whets consumer appetite for products, handles thousands of calls a minute via its computerized answering service, and maintains a minute-by-minute gauge of sales data that is made available to on-camera salespersons. This allows an ever-changing sales pitch to promote what sells the most. The network viewer interested in a product being sold has only to dial a toll-free telephone number, provide all necessary mailing information, and give a valid credit card number. Within days, the product is delivered to the home.

In 1993, two separate events impacted strongly on the growth and direction of home shopping services.

First, the Federal Communications Commission voted to require cable television operators to carry the signals of local broadcasting that run home shopping programs twenty-four hours a day and stated that such broadcasts are in the public interest.

This decision immediately opened a vast new market outlet to retailers nationwide, who recognize that home shopping services (presently some seventy different operations throughout the country) are a strong potential source of sales revenue, one that requires educated and motivated salespeople to be their personal representative to newly established sales territories. At the same time, specialty outlets, mass-merchandising merchants, department store chains, and catalog retailers have begun evaluating and planning how best to use the home shopping channels for their individual products/services.

Secondly, Home Shopping Network, Inc., the firm that pioneered what in 1993 was a two to three billion dollar a year industry, and QVC Network, Inc., the other major home shopping operation, announced plans to merge—a move that would create a multibillion-dollar home shopping network available to more than two-thirds of all television households and encompassing some 99 percent of all home-shopping markets.

Prior to this merger, each firm presented its products via a distinct on-camera sales style that demanded versatility and quick adaptation to market needs. Now, regardless of their former on-camera format, the merged networks' influence will continue to be strongly felt throughout the retail world, challenging retailers to change their individual television shopping service methods, advertising, and market outlook to effectively compete in today's marketplace.

Interactive

The anticipated opportunities needed for retailers to successfully compete via interactive television began taking effect in 1994. From wireless communication received by handheld computers to vehicle dashboard screens, viewers will be able to communicate with sales programs/outlets through their television sets—using a combination of a control box (available for a monthly fee) and their set's remote control. They will examine specific merchandise, request additional visual/verbal information, select goods of their choice, place their order, and make payment at one time. Ultimately, it is expected that consumers will talk directly to those doing the selling.

Five hundred cable television channels have been added to provide retailers with access to an ever growing market where they can promote their products twenty-four hours a day. It is anticipated that this will create increasingly intense competition for the current home-shopping services, infomercials, pay-per-view movies, entertainment and sports events, and the growing availability of specialty areas (banking, stock market, medical services, etc.) already using cable television. Today's salesperson will find ever expanding opportunities to conceive, develop, produce, market, and follow-up with specific and innovative sales programs and procedures toward the growing market of interactive television.

Local and national merchants will have to find the right spokesperson for their product, develop successful sales messages, determine the best selling hours and sales force, and maintain consumer interest in their offerings through innovative technology capable of soliciting, receiving, and processing customer orders on a timely basis. All such changes will influence advertising, the manufacture of consumer goods, and the nation's total economy as new retailing and sales needs come to be redefined.

Infomercials

Infomercials (information plus commercial), with yearly sales of billions of dollars, were initially thirty-minute presentations found during television's unappealing late night, early morning, or Saturday afternoon hours, often disguised as news, game, or talk shows. Today they are moving into prime-time slots as television stations are more willing to sell thirty-minute blocks for commercial purposes. The infomercial, which builds corporate images, educates consumers, and complements retail products already on store shelves, also offers their creators several positive selling advantages not available within the confines of today's standard television advertising.

Economical   The cost to produce a thirty-minute infomercial is comparable to the cost of producing a thirty-second television commercial. The technical skills on display in television advertisements are no longer lacking in the majority of infomercials, as competition requires quality production to reach and hold potential customers. The infomercial's looser format, carefully programmed by skilled salespeople, brings together successful entertainers, business professionals, and recognized social entrepreneurs to promote the product with greater emphasis.

Explanatory   There are times a sponsor cannot effectively explain the purpose, intricacy, uniqueness, and/or benefits of its product in a thirty- or sixty-second television commercial. The infomercial, which uses a variety of professional sales techniques and personnel, provides time for in-depth discussion, practical demonstration/explanation, and a full-scale viewer promotion supported by successful public figures.

Responsive   Infomercials often have a direct response opportunity that allows viewers to call a toll-free telephone number to order the product. This provides the seller with immediate sales leads while allowing the viewer/customer to obtain additional information, talk with the show's hosts and guests, or give personal testimony concerning the product. Such instantaneous feedback cannot be obtained from the standard television commercial—regardless of how many times that commercial is run!

TELEMARKETING

Another expanding source of successful selling is telemarketing—the electronic version of the door-to-door salesperson. It provides solicitation by telephone to sell a product, support a cause, endorse individuals/organizations, offer services, or promote social agendas while soliciting financial contributions or payments for services offered.

Telemarketing, to its critics, is an unwarranted intrusion into the privacy of telephone owners. To its supporters and users, telemarketing is a quick, efficient, and timesaving means of reaching the widest possible market for the minimum outlay of time and dollars.

Recent court decisions have restructured the computerized form of telemarketing, which used sophisticated computers, automatically dialed telephones, and a recorded sales message that allowed the recipient, if interested, to record his or her name, address, and a personal message if desired. Now there are "predictive dialers"—units that ring many telephone numbers simultaneously but, when a call is answered, switches that call to an operator (who can give a live presentation or play a prerecorded message).

Telemarketing is the first major telephone marketing industry that has the capability to target potential customers by every demographic applicable to the product being sold. It is anticipated that in the future telemarketing will include television screen linkup to its system, giving recipients a full menu of available products, ordering requirements, and other information. At the same time, miniature fax machines will transmit receipts and additional product information to the customer.

COMPUTERS

The computer is a significant and growing tool in attaining successful sales. Salespeople in all areas have available, at affordable prices, a wide variety of portable computers to make their daily workload quicker, easier, and more effective than in the past.

Recognizing this, many companies provide their sales force with the latest in computer systems to assist in tracking customers, maintaining necessary paperwork, preparing and presenting sales information to customers, giving faster and more effective responses to customers' requests, and having up-to-date corporate and manufacturing data at hand on a daily basis.

At the same time, the rise in home computer use is challenging retailers and sales personnel at all levels to "produce or perish," i.e., to develop innovative sales techniques that will draw the customer away from his or her home and computer and into the sales environment.

Computer Shopping Services

A sales concept similar to that in the telemarketing field is offered by competing computer shopping services, which provide an opportunity for customers to shop through an "electronic mall." For a yearly membership fee and/or a per-minute line charge, customers (subscribers) need only a personal computer, a modem, some specially prepared software, and a credit card. As members, they are offered a wide range of products and services: discounts (from 10 to 15 percent) on goods purchased, participation in service-sponsored contests, receipt of a monthly magazine (movie reviews, financial information, etc.), and, at participating stores, an available charge account activated by home computer. In the process, the shopper avoids moving from store to store, parking, traffic congestion, wasted time, and emotional upset. Retailers benefit through reduced stock on hand, lowered maintenance and store inventories, fewer sales personnel, and less advertising efforts to draw customers.

This change in sales direction becomes a challenge to retailers and salespeople at all levels to develop new means and methods to acquire and maintain personal customer sales.

To better develop and serve this market, on-line services have upgraded every area of customer interest into a more "interactive" relationship that will blend home-shopping channels with the widening range of on-line services.

Company-to-Company

Computers today are a boon to the manufacturing process. They are capable of initiating orders from Company A to Company B; of receiving, filing, and shipping orders; of maintaining and replenishing stocks; and of recording, reporting, and filing all associated paperwork.

A manufacturer's established customers can be connected via computer modem with the firm's own computer to allow for their daily material orders, depending on current needs. Though certainly this electronic communicating benefits the buyer's day-to-day operations, it remains for the salesperson to be there in person with hands-on knowledge to interpret and explain new product innovations, company procedures, buyer's objectives, and how it all can work efficiently for the success of both sides as the seller.

Computer Retailing

Retail sales firms, feeling the impact of television and telemarketing campaigns on their daily business, have brought computers into everyday operations in a massive effort to maintain and increase sales opportunities and success.

Within some national grocery store chains, customers can link their home computers via modem with the mainframe computer at the chain's corporate headquarters. From this, subscribers can shop for more than fifteen thousand items within the chain's stores. Customers are able to obtain goods that fit their exact needs through the system's detailed, aisle-by-aisle, menu. Once ordered, subscribers beam their orders to the store where "pickers" do the physical shopping and deliver the assembled order to the customers' homes. At the same time, the computer system continually updates prices and product information and oversees special cash registers within the store's checkout area.

Grocery stores nationwide are incorporating such computer-directed services: product shelves that talk; electronic checkout systems that dispense coupons and play commercials; overhead electronic billboards that promote product information; shopping carts with built-in television screens that offer buying recommendations; blinking lights on coupon dispensers; and television monitors at the checkout stand that run product commercials or provide local news information.

These computer activities, developed to increase sales through easing customer time and travel in shopping, are augmented by growing links between customer, retailer, and the financial institutions, which allow customer payments to immediately be credited to the retailer's accounts.

As more and more households acquired home personal computers, the interlinking—customers to retailers to banks—has expanded greatly, allowing the individual to do more business and shopping and payment activities from their home with ever increasing opportunities for greater access to goods and services. This has become an ever expanding and positive challenge for sales personnel everywhere. Not only must they effectively represent their firm to the public with increased knowledge, promotional skills, and a positive personality toward all individuals, they must also continue to fulfill their basic role within the ever growing global marketing system.

SALES ENGINEERS

Sales engineers are usually employed by manufacturers and are highly knowledgeable in the technical aspects of the product. They create, design, and promote specific programs to resolve company-based problems.

The sales engineer position often requires advanced college training in such complex fields as engineering (B.S.E. degree), metallurgy, and computer integrity. The sales engineer has to be creative, inventive, and able to relate well to technical demands of the chosen specialty, and yet be able to get along with others not technically oriented with whom they work or meet in their day-to-day activity.

A sales engineer is a pioneer on the cutting edge of society. What is discovered, developed, marketed, sold, and serviced by these experts today will, at the present rate of technological growth, be run-of-the-mill material for future salespersons within a few years.

A CAUTIONARY NOTE

As in all growth industries, there will be found a small percentage of individuals interested only in the exploitation of others for profit. These individuals use the media to sell inferior goods or, after accepting viewer orders, will fail to deliver promised products or provide satisfaction.

The sales newcomer seriously considering applying his or her talents to any sales area should carefully review the specific job opportunity offered, its personnel, past performance, credit rating, growth potential, and overall customer response before becoming actively committed to the business.

SERVICE AND RESPONSIBILITIES

Now that you have had a chance to study the many sales positions available and determine which you prefer, the next question must be: What must I now do to prepare myself for my chosen selling career? The following sections will review the basic steps needed. Responsibility is as necessary to success as dependability and self-discipline. Without personal responsibility in several specific areas within sales, standard careers available will offer little of the pleasure or the experiences career paths may provide.

In light of ever growing public awareness, organizations demand the highest standards in manufacturing and production procedures. Personal conduct, business ethics, advertising, and promotional efforts all are so important that such activities are now the business norm rather than the exception.

Responsibility to the Company

The company is the provider of products and/or services, personnel, research, advertising and promotional efforts, use of company car, expense account (including mileage and other automotive expenses, lodging, meals, laundry and dry cleaning, customer entertainment, telephone service, tips, and miscellaneous materials), supplies as needed, relocation expenses (in many cases), medical and dental insurance, holiday pay, bonuses, and other benefits such as educational and technical training courses.

This company investment provides opportunities for abuse by irresponsible persons. At the same time, the responsible salesperson will strive to recognize the benefits of ethical conduct and will studiously avoid any such improprieties.

Representing the Company   A salesperson is often the front edge of a firm's contact with the customer. He or she bears the responsibility of representing the firm in as accurate and honest a manner as possible. This means not creating false images of self-importance at company expense; not developing production and/or personnel records that are misleading or false; and not making under-the-table deals with customers for personal gain.

The customer must be able to trust the salesperson. Through such trust the company gains respect and confidence from the buyer. This cannot happen unless the salesperson acts in an accurate and honest manner, which creates mutual goodwill.

In specific company areas, the salesperson should develop responsibility, ethics, and integrity.

Dealing with Fellow Salespeople   At times company-assigned territories can overlap. Then those salespeople involved should come together and cooperatively resolve any problems. In this manner, no customer becomes the arguing point of two determined salespeople promoting the same products in different ways at the expense of one another. In smaller situations (for instance, a large department store or an auto dealership), company policy should be in place to prevent one salesperson from taking credit for the effort of another. If there is no policy established, it is the responsibility of those involved to develop guidelines for specific situations and to adhere to them.

Product Use   There could be a temptation, depending on the company products, to use them for personal needs. At times, companies will encourage such use at no cost. This allows the salespeople to experience firsthand how the product is used and enhance their knowledge of the product so they can best deal with customers who will experience the same positive and negative results of the product.

In other cases, the company may not want its product removed from the sales market simply to satisfy a salesperson's need. Such a view also may extend to company supplies and materials (stationery, postage, office equipment) not to be used for personal business.

The responsible salesperson can easily recognize the fine line between serving the company and serving the self at company expense. Thus, the responsible salesperson will act according to the best interests and goals of the company.

Expense Sheet (Reports) The temptation and opportunity to increase on-the-road costs through the expense account is always available to the salesperson. There is little a company can do to prove mark-ups of expenses. Receipts can be altered, created, or taken from other sources.

It is an indication of ethical laxity in the salesperson to indulge in this form of stealing. If the individual is caught "padding" the expense account, the loss of his or her job and all associated benefits, plus the burden of carrying the stigma throughout the rest of one's career, is just not worth it. No matter how clever someone thinks he or she might be, that person will eventually be revealed as a thief, a description not exactly appealing to prospective future employers.

Certainly, if the salesperson's income, including commissions and other bonuses, is insufficient, the company has a responsibility to correct the situation. If not, the salesperson has a responsibility to herself or himself to confront the employer openly with a request for increased compensation or else seek a more rewarding position.

If, however, the financial factors are equal or better than the industry average, it can only mean the salesperson has deliberately abdicated responsibility to the company for self-interest. In such a case, the company will take appropriate and immediate action.

Company Car The company car is a separate responsibility involving many areas and cannot be treated with indifference. Though the itemizing of all company-related expenses is a test of the salesperson's honesty and responsibility, the commitment to others on the road is an even greater value.

The salesperson is in a unique position when behind the wheel of the company car. He or she not only is the representative of the firm and required to act appropriately and safely, but also is expected to assure those around him or her of safe intentions. If a salesperson, through irresponsibility, causes an accident, the victims will turn to the "deep pockets" of the company for compensation. The company, through its insurance agent, will wind up paying all bills, damages, lawsuits, legal fees, and other associated costs.

When a company has placed its trust in its sales representative, the representative must repay that trust with responsible action.

Benefits   In addition to major medical health insurance and life insurance policies, most companies now provide additional benefits for their employees. These may include tuition reimbursement, paid sick days and holidays, reimbursement of moving expenses, health club memberships, and on and on. Prior to actually going to work for a company, it is always a good idea to determine exactly how extensive the corporation's benefit plan is and what, if any, cost the employee is expected to pay.

Responsibility to the Competition

Competition, more than any other social and economic factor in business, has raised product standards, enhanced manufacturing criteria, and improved sales performance and presentation.

A salesperson seeks to outdo the competition by highlighting her or his firm's product's virtues. However, good sales representatives do not downgrade the competition as a means of promoting their own products. This is a sign of poor salesmanship that many times produces the opposite reaction in a buyer.

Customers require subtle servicing. They seek the best product with the most assurances and guarantees at the lowest price. That is what their job requires them to find, and that is why so many salespeople pass through their doors. Understanding this, salespeople seek to find opportunities to get a leg up on their competition. They do so by selling their product more aggressively and with heightened awareness of the superiority of their product over the competition.

The simple ethical attitudes a salesperson will take in dealing with competitive claims include the following:

Compare Honestly If the competition has a similar product, the salesperson does not abuse ethics by pointing out the competition's weaknesses against her or his more qualified product. It becomes irresponsibility when pointing out becomes malicious condemnation without justification.

Recommend Openly If the salesperson's product cannot meet customer demand or need, the responsible salesperson will not hesitate to recommend a competitor whose product might well fill the demand. Such a gesture allows the customer access to additional sources not otherwise known to satisfy immediate needs. It also strengthens the original salesperson's position with that customer ("I can depend on this person to help me when I need help, even at the cost of her or his own sale"). This increases customer respect and appreciation ("I owe you one").

Help One Another Besides the example above, salespeople have the opportunity to help one another in many ways.

Friendships outside of business hours have been developed on the road, where two or more salespeople come together to discuss tactics, products, customer needs, and sales goals. More importantly, there can be days (there always are) when nothing seems right—the customer went fishing, the product malfunctioned, no orders were written—but the sense of frustration and discouragement can be lifted quickly when the positive and enthusiastic attitudes of a fellow toiler in the vineyards turn the negatives around toward tomorrow's opportunities.

Responsibility to the Customer

The most important information needed by the manufacturer's salespeople is their customer's bottom line—how much money will that firm spend annually on company needs?

Less than a decade ago, costs directed to company needs by the top one hundred industrial spenders ranged as high as half a trillion dollars. By the mid 1990s, industrial America was undergoing a transformation—downsizing, reorganization/consolidation, and work distributed among fewer employees. According to the U.S. Department of Labor, this trend resulted in America's manufacturing workers putting in an average of 4.4 hours of overtime per week.

With a smaller workforce, increased technological innovations that enhance and improve production, and more knowledgeable management decisions of and toward company success (profits), money allocated to company needs has been steadily reduced.

Though companies will tend to spend less on specific needs, what money is available will serve as catalyst to the manufacturer's salespeople, whose job it is to locate the markets and promote goods and services to them.

For the retail salesperson and others, the financial figure is based on available consumer capital, which rises or falls based on business, economic, national, and international fluctuations. Whatever particular sales area you choose, there is a commitment of responsibility to the customer served.

Many selling techniques previously considered tried-and-true (unrealistic product claims, deceptive guarantees, high-pressure methods) have been discarded for openness and a cooperative approach. Today's salesperson must effectively determine what the customer wants and needs, the best means to provide it, what tools will be needed for the sales effort (advertising, promotional sheets, incentives, giveaways), means of delivery, how to handle damaged or rejected products, and the reordering process.

Under such action guidelines, the salesperson is guided by personal involvement with the customer and the individual responsibility to that customer in a number of areas.

The Product   The immediate reason a salesperson seeks out the company buyer is to sell the product. We have indicated that the most valuable asset any salesperson can develop is a climate of customer confidence and trust. This means the customer must be provided with correct, updated, and factual information detailing all aspects of the product, sales terms, order conditions, delivery dates, guarantees, servicing available, and many other specific items.

The perceptive salesperson will understand that the product will stand or fall *not* on a sales presentation but under actual working conditions. If the customer has been "sold," the product must equal or excel the salesperson's realistic presentation claims. If it does not, that salesperson will risk creating a dissatisfied customer who will look elsewhere for more truthful and dependable product representation.

Scheduling   The customer orders goods based on specific company plans. The products needed for those plans will be expected at specific times. The committed salesperson sees to it that those goods arrive on or before the assigned delivery time. In an emergency, the salesperson provides the time, effort, and personal knowledge to ensure that the products needed are delivered by the fastest available means.

This aspect of the sales effort, involving both the salesperson and other company personnel, builds customer satisfaction and enhances the image of dependability by which most companies and their salespeople succeed.

Legality   There are two forms of illegal actions that must be immediately and responsibly dealt with when encountered by the salesperson.

In some situations the salesperson may find it difficult, if not impossible, to successfully avoid complicity in these illegal actions. Still, every effort must be made to maintain responsible conduct in the handling of reciprocity and bribery.

Reciprocity.   The idea is simple: Firm A will only buy its needed goods from Firm B *if* Firm B will only buy its needed goods from Firm A.

This type of "sweetheart" agreement, never verbalized or put into writing, negates the salesperson's purpose and relegates her or him to nothing more than an order taker. At the same time, reciprocity is advocated by some sales types as a financial gold mine (lower costs overall, ease of paperwork, continuation of plant-to-plant relationships). It is, however, a means of cutting off access to individual companies by outsiders and, as a company policy, should be brought to an end wherever found.

Bribery.   The reality of bribery is hard to recognize these days as it has become so subtle. Gone, for the most part, is the direct-cash payment to get some action taken. Now bribes come in all shapes and forms: a night on the town, season tickets to major sporting or social events, special parties, discreet but overly expensive gifts, long weekend getaways, and other particular favors.

The responsiblity to the customer can be challenged, if not completely terminated, by a customer's solicitation of such goodies. It is even worse when the salesperson, with company approval, offers such fringe benefits to the customer (with the understanding between both of what price the customer must pay).

There is a fine line between the transferring of gifts in business situations (with gift, gift price, and means of giving relevant to the appropriate occasion), but the unethical giving for which greater "gifts" are expected in return (a *quid pro quo*) remains an unwelcomed, but too-often present, part of doing business.

When such a situation arises, the person being offered an obvious bribe must take the responsibility for immediate termination of the relationship and report such efforts to both company and legal officials.

Today many firms forbid buyers at any level to accept gifts above a certain cash value (for example, $25). Some companies have examined the situation and simply said "no" to any gift of any kind for any employee, especially their buyers. In such cases, if a supplier is discovered to have violated that rule, the company will terminate its association with that supplier indefinitely.

REQUIREMENTS FOR SELLING

As you have seen, there are many sales areas and many sellers' responsibilities. Once you have selected the type of sales area that offers you the greatest challenges and rewards and you can accept the critical areas of personal responsibility, it is time to begin work on the basic requirements needed to begin selling.

What You Are Selling

This is a subtle issue with many answers, each a vital part for individual success.

You Sell a Product   To sell any product properly, you must *know* it as thoroughly and intimately as though you had made it yourself, step by step. In this knowledge, you cannot only detail all capabilities of the product to a customer, but also provide accurate disassembly and reassembly if required as demonstration of product merit. Such familiarity allows you to put together a presentation based on this knowledge, and that provides a sense of inner confidence (in the product and in yourself) that is easily transmitted to the buyer.

Knowing what the product can and cannot do (features and benefits) allows you flexibility in providing positive recommendations to enhance the operations of the customer's firm by new applications of the product.

You Sell Your Personality   Your personality will help open business doors in the first months of your new career. After that, recognition and confidence formed through your conduct and actions will do the trick.

After all, looking good in appearance and feeling good inside will make you radiate confidence about the product. Your customer should see you looking your best. Your attitude has much to do with your outward personality and your relationship with others. It won't matter if you have a well-practiced smile, warm eyes, standing-tall stance, clean haircut, pressed suit, shined shoes, and excellent posture if your personality reflects selfish, surly, and sarcastic responses to those around you.

The primary qualities salespeople must convey are sincerity, confidence, dependability, responsibility, knowledge, and a personal interest in the other person—in this case, the customer. With such qualities, selling is more than 50 percent completed. With only one or two, you might be interested in sales, but your success probability is near zero.

You Sell Solutions   The product you provide is simply a solution to the buyer's company's problems. It may be office supplies, machine parts, medical stocks, or any other item or service used by others to correct problems or maintain daily operations.

The creative salesperson armed with the right product and a pleasing personality is expected to know the necessary solutions to what a customer seeks, but more is required.

Understanding Customer and Competition

The innovative salesperson needs to know everything about individual customers (operations, goals, personnel, attitudes, past performance, financial rating, management organization, social structure, surroundings, areas of influence, and political position). The seller must know every detail so as to provide in-depth information and service based on knowledge utilized to enhance and further the corporate goals and purposes for the customer.

He or she needs to know everything available on the competition (personnel, sales staff, programs, pricing, manufacturing rates, shipping facilities, delivery times and methods, special promotions and offers, particular products, and incentive programs). The salesperson needs to know every bit of information that will allow for a more knowledgeable sales effort, from formulation to presentation.

Effective Communication Skills

Without the ability to present ideas, insights, and information clearly and effectively through communications, a salesperson would never succeed. To communicate is to open another's mind to the realms within one's own mind, and those areas, carefully prepared, are the salesperson's best chance for success.

To do this, the salesperson must overcome the inner reluctance of the buyer. The buyer must be enticed to listen and become interested, then enthused, then confident in the decision to buy.

Many salespeople, in approaching customers, have prepared their meeting with one of communication's more effective prescriptions for success:

- *Tell them what you will tell them:* Explain what the subject is and how it will be presented;

- *Tell them:* Present all information in a factual and informative way with opportunities for questions and further explanations and information;
- *Tell them what you just told them:* Review the entire presentation to ensure that every person understood the material, and solicit additional questions.

Such reinforcement of the sales message strengthens the customer's commitment to the product and enhances the salesperson's communicative ability through providing information, support materials, and product knowledge in triplicate.

Another sales adage is: "You have to tell it well to sell it well."

There are dozens of books available through local libraries and bookstores on the "how-to" of public speaking. These lessons, incorporated into sales presentations, will create marked improvement in promoting the message, acquiring additional self-confidence, and adapting present skills to higher performance levels.

The major emphasis of successful communications is that of a two-way, give-and-take-affair. The salesperson presents the product information plus all related materials. Then the customer asks relevant questions, responses are made by the salesperson, decisions are reached, and both sides have shown the power of creative communications.

It is easy to recognize the value of communications but what, specifically, makes it work?

Speaking Skills   "The object of oratory," claims Macaulay in *The Athenian Orators,* "is not truth, but persuasion." The sales representative's presentation, if given with Macaulay in mind, is the major step toward buyer acceptance or rejection. If given in a monotone, with hesitations, stammerings, and word bridges (errr, ummm, you know, all right, OK, uh-huh) between sentences, such a presentation will fail. With its failure will fall the salesperson. When, however, the individual selling is obviously enthusiastic, speaks clearly and to the point, interjects appropriate silent pauses, is sincere, and reflects personal knowledge of the product and buyer, the sale is very close to completion.

Most people feel secure listening to well-tempered, melodic voices that, rather than presenting simple facts, add emotional and visual images to the presentation. Word pictures are created that help establish the buyer's mood for the presentation.

A salesperson should be able to *enunciate* words (speak so that each sound is clearly understood) and, in so doing, ensure that all words receive the proper *pronunciation* (making each word clear in presentation).

The beginning salesperson intent on improving communication skills should have a cassette tape recorder available and use it at every opportunity. By putting the sales presentation on tape (either as practice or during an actual effort) and listening with critical ears, the problems that buyers heard and responded to negatively will very quickly be realized and can be corrected.

The salesperson must consider the following questions about the sales presentation:

1. Are there run-on words? ("Diyadoit?" instead of "Did you do it?")
2. Are letters dropped from words? ("Goin'" for "going" or "livin'" for "living")
3. Are there appropriate pauses?
4. Is the voice flat and monotonous, or does it reflect enthusiasm with variety of pitch and tone?
5. Do spoken "s"-letters come out with a hiss?
6. Was there adequate emphasis of particular information to be highlighted?
7. Is the voice speaking too fast or slow?

8. Is the voice intimidating, friendly, or bored?
9. Are there delays at the end of sentences to allow the buyer to comment if necessary?
10. Does laughter highlight the presentation at appropriate moments?

To improve the presentation speech further, salespeople should employ the following techniques:

1. Use visually colorful words.
2. Use words to convey specific meaning. If not clear, discuss the meaning as part of the presentation.
3. Weigh words carefully before using them. Recognize the listener's views, beliefs, and attitudes.
4. Use emotional words that stir the listener and help visualize what's being said.
5. Personalize the presentation to the buyer's interests—that is, company, home, family, or community.

Most people, when listening to others, will appreciate appropriate humor and references that make them feel more comfortable. Which of the following lines would work more effectively with a buyer of rock quarry supplies: "This product uses little gas in daily operations," or "This product drinks gas like a rock absorbs water"?

If you guessed the second statement, you would be like the majority of listeners—and you would be in error. A quarry owner, following a heavy downpour of several hours, would be firmly convinced that rocks hold water (some actually do) and would think only of the work delay and problems created by water-logged land and rock beds.

In today's technological world, the average person may recognize some six thousand independent words, use perhaps one thousand in daily conversations, and come across the others only sporadically. By reading—books, magazines, trade journals, house organs, Sunday supplements, general-interest promotional materials, journals, reports, and research papers—any individual can quickly increase word recognition and use.

A successful project that will increase word skills uses a dictionary. Pick any word—noun, pronoun, adjective, adverb—and list it on paper under Column One. Then list in Column Two beside it all synonyms provided. Then in Column Three list all synonyms you find for those words in Column Two, and continue in this manner as far as possible. If lucky in your original word choice, you will have found a word that expands your word knowledge, rather than closes it off.

An example to start practice in learning words can be:

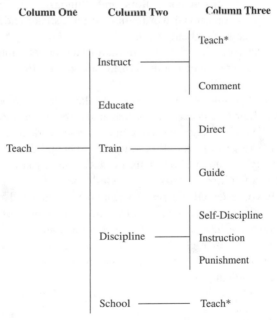

Column One	Column Two	Column Three
		Teach*
	Instruct	
		Comment
	Educate	
		Direct
Teach	Train	
		Guide
		Self-Discipline
	Discipline	Instruction
		Punishment
	School	Teach*

*indicates comparable word elsewhere or no listed synonyms

Effective verbal communications are the salesperson's main strength in projecting the message to others.

Listening Skills   This is the most important sales skill. If he or she lacks the time or interest to listen, the salesperson misses valuable information and important guidelines for future activities relative to the customer. There is always sufficient time to listen. It is estimated that an individual listens about four times faster than a person talks. This provides the listener with time to think, to prepare answers, to concentrate on specific points, and sometimes to miss most of what's being said because the listener is thinking rather than listening!

Listening is critical to success. To improve on this vital skill, a salesperson can develop individual programs that include a personal and concentrated interest in what's being said and the ability to organize and arrange responses rather than trying to interrupt the speaker. There should be an awareness of what points can be retained for future benefit and a oneness with the speaker to feel and absorb the information as it is given.

Visual Aids in Communications   Many salespeople use the product, information sheets, charts, graphs, photographs, artwork, film strips, slide shows, computer-generated presentations, and other materials to illustrate and explain their product, its performance, and purpose. This requires the ability to organize the presentation so that the verbal information flows with, and becomes one with, the visual materials. It allows the buyer as audience to be swept away within an intelligent, verbalized, enthusiastic, and sincere presentation, the sole purpose of which is to provide the buyer with satisfaction through the salesperson's message.

Self-Discipline

We briefly discussed self-discipline earlier, but it will not hurt to restate its importance to a successful sales career. In most sales positions, the salesperson is often on her or his own. Direct supervision usually is not immediately available. When needed, a supervisor can be contacted by telephone to clarify information or provide higher authorization.

Such an open work schedule tempts some employees to follow a policy of "Always put off until tomorrow what you can avoid doing today."

It means: Don't wake up early and start working. Don't telephone customers. Don't write orders or other business. Don't read trade journals or keep up on the latest information within the field. Don't do homework or communications or paperwork required by the company.

It also means: Don't expect to be a salesperson for very long.

Self-discipline is the salesperson's first act toward success. It keeps the individual *doing,* regardless of inner feelings and attitudes. It ensures that the extra telephone calls will be made, the necessary paperwork will be completed, and the programs and presentations will be worked on that much harder.

The self-disciplined salesperson does not need a time-schedule at the job, because all the time available is to be directed toward company success. Such commitment to a sales position is only as strong as the self-discipline that the job and its opportunities ignite within the salesperson.

Organization and Time Management

The salesperson interested in professional advancement within the sales ranks will quickly learn the truth of management's viewpoint that an organized schedule is the sign of an organized mind. That, of course, is what proper organization must be.

The salesperson on the job must be able mentally to adapt to diverse conditions through careful implementation of sometimes apparently spontaneous actions. Though such flexibility might seem to be in contradiction to the rigidity of proper organization, the opposite is actually true.

Two terms, at this point, must be defined. *Organization* is the arrangement of all forces touching the salesperson's activities into a workable whole. *Management* is the actual implementation of specific activities found on the organization table.

Salespeople, like those in managerial positions, can effectively organize the day's activities down to the last second. Such organization can be an example for all to see. But if those people have little or no management ability, such organization is meaningless, because it is not acted upon in the best manner— if at all.

A salesperson's daily activities are varied, including sales meetings and demonstrations, entertainment, meals, office or on-the-road paperwork, correspondence, and presentation improvements. These are but some of the situations that must be properly organized and aligned for expedient action.

Such organization includes determining the relative importance of each activity; placement of each activity, by importance, on a daily work schedule; and following the schedule to complete as many activities listed as possible. Those *not* completed on Day 1 go to the top of the Day 2 list.

Thorough organization of activities on paper, allowing a visual comparison of what has to be done, enhances the workday by ensuring that what must be done will be done.

In 1746, Benjamin Franklin wrote in *Poor Richard's Almanac:* "Don't thou love life? Then do not squander time, for that's the stuff life is made of." Salespeople learn this message very quickly.

There are many books available on proper time management principles and procedures, detailed "how-to" works by which the individual's entire daily life can be run by stopwatch. There are motivational seminars, in-depth educational programs, and in-plant training materials highlighting proper time-management principles for all.

In essence, the salesperson confronted by the desire to control time is given three basic steps toward that goal:

1. Establish priorities. List what is important toward company and personal goals (criteria that must be met in each area of activity) and arrange all items by number rank, the most important being Number One.
2. Complete priorities. Start at Number One and work downward, completing each specific item as quickly and efficiently as possible.
3. Prepare next day's priorities. Repeat the steps for the first list as needed, then incorporate appropriately items from that list not completed today.

Self-organization, based on flexible time-management efforts to ensure that time is neither wasted nor abused, will quickly become one of the salesperson's strongest pillars of support.

Servicing

Though the salesperson is the "point" of the company's advance on customers and their facilities, he or she must often work "cleanup" once entrance has been gained and the order given.

Call-backs, stop-bys, and necessary calls for consultation and advice sought by the customer will bring the salesperson in touch with a greater variety of company employees and interests. In this way he or she provides the knowledge of product operation, maintenance, and support while benefiting from the knowledge and support of the customer's staff.

Locating New Prospects

Most sales positions today allow time for prospecting—contacting and visiting new companies to introduce the salesperson's product, self, and other material. In assigning territories, many companies expect this conduct. Often a sales representative moving outside his or her territory into areas where no other company sales rep has gone will advance the company's interests and, in so doing, increase the assigned territory in which to sell. Such efforts, usually with company approval and support (to ensure no conflict with others) require only a telephone book to locate potential customers.

There are continual challenges for the salesperson today, from customers, competition, creators (of products newer and better than those currently available), and self.

Each force acting upon the sales representative enhances the ability to expand sales techniques further and involves the careful preparation of the salesperson to deal with the ever-changing buying world.

CHAPTER 4

SALES MANAGEMENT

"All great changes are irksome to the human mind, especially those which are attended with great dangers and uncertain effects."

John Adams
Letter to James Warren

The main purpose of sales management is to raise the total profit by each salesperson, provide customers greater product value and service, and provide salespeople with the opportunity to maximize personal income and growth.

Sales management within a business (manufacturing, industrial, retail, or other) is responsible for the distribution of company products and services. The sales manager is responsible for company sales goals, maintenance, and sales force direction (including all training), as well as having review authority over all salespeople's daily activities and accomplishments to guarantee success.

THE DIFFERENCE BETWEEN SALES
MANAGEMENT AND ACTUAL SELLING

The sales manager overseeing the sales force either has been brought up from the sales ranks or hired from outside the company

69

at high expense. As a salesperson, he or she probably held the company's highest sales records and often had its greatest sales experience. When the promotion of such a person succeeds, it is to the company's credit, though it does lose its best salesperson from the selling ranks. When the individual selected is not successful as a sales manager, it usually is because that individual is unable to handle the management aspects required, and the company will suffer.

The salesperson is skilled in successful selling techniques, self-management, and dealing with individual customers one-on-one. The sales manager is skilled in providing guidance and motivation to the total sales staff, developing successful sales programs, establishing sales goals, and overseeing all aspects of sales force activity as it relates to company sales.

MANAGING THE SALES FORCE

The successful salesperson *can* become a successful sales manager through the deliberate development of corporate goals and the successful application of the basic principles demanded of the sales job.

Knowledge

The sales manager must know the company's goals (long- and short-term), financial structure, credit rating, operational procedures, management, decision-making process, individual departments and department heads, product research, distribution and receiving processes, and all related areas that add to knowledge already in place. In the same light, the successful sales manager will learn the same information about each competitor, thus allowing the development of sound and workable sales programs.

Added to this is the personal knowledge gained as a salesperson of company products, production schedules, prices (including discounts, warranties, and guarantees), delivery routes and methods, incentives, advertising and promotional plans, follow-up ideas, customer relations, and the personnel of the employer, as well as those of the competition.

While serving as a salesperson within an assigned territory, the sales manager was able to meet and coordinate sales programs and presentations with other salespeople within the company. Now the limited information available from fellow salespersons has to be increased as much as possible. This means knowing the personal habits, individual characteristics, hidden attitudes, and long-range outlooks for each salesperson. Such awareness is used to maximize that individual's production (sales) by one-on-one discussions, personal recommendations, and an interest beyond the company's goals.

Ability

Although the sales manager needs many of the same skills as a salesperson, what makes a highly successful salesperson will not always make a successful sales manager.

Personal abilities gained as a salesperson should include the ability to communicate orally and in print. Whether speaking to one or one thousand or writing a brief thank-you note, communication allows others to recognize the sales manager who is informed, involved, and inspired.

A special skill vital to the sales manager's success is recognizing and acting upon personal instincts. In making quick decisions when dealing with others, there is no room for self-doubt concerning such decisions. Bovee put it best by stating: "Doubt whom you will, but never yourself."

Since the sales manager is responsible for the success or failure of company sales programs, he or she must be successful in knowing new salespeople or applicants, planning individualized or company training programs, and evaluating daily activity, field reports, customer responses, and fellow salespeople's insights, while providing appropriate recognition and constructive criticism as needed.

A sales manager possessing the necessary qualities is recognized by the presence of a smooth-running sales force; excellent intercompany relationships with department heads, executive management, and hourly employees; and an increased customer relations and services output. Such positive results are created through the varied abilities of the sales manager.

Intelligence   A sales manager unable to think intelligently cannot hope to find success. Intelligence, directed toward others and based on inner factors (reason, logic, common sense, compassion) requires an emotional, business, professional, and personal makeup that will deal effectively, but fairly, with all issues, personalities, and problems.

People Handling   A good sales manager, no matter how physically or emotionally drained or hurt, must always instill and encourage in others a personal sense of well-being from within. This is seen by others as self-confidence and self-assurance. Such leadership does not rely on anger or negative emotions but on the inherent good within people.

At the same time, the sales manager must be able to deal quickly and fairly with inside-the-company issues, where he or she is expected to make immediate decisions to enhance the company image and progress. In so doing, salespeople are dealt with on a one-on-one basis with total support or discipline given within a nonjudgmental atmosphere.

The effective sales manager also knows the appropriate use of praise, making a wholesome effort to give the salesperson as much credit as possible and to refrain from taking credit for himself or herself when it is not due.

When a sales manager's staff recognizes her or him as a boss who will support their actions to management and mete out punishment fairly when needed, there will be a willingness to give total commitment to the company.

Flexibility   Every sale made and every salesperson responsible for that sale is unique. The sales manager who takes time to recognize this will not tamper with a working and successful program. He or she will recognize that each salesperson is an individual and that an individual's personal style has much to do with developing and presenting her or his program.

The rigid "by-the-book" sales manager soon learns that going by the book often leads to disaster. Each presentation and salesperson must be flexible and able to incorporate the combined skills, attitudes, knowledge, and experience of the salesperson and sales manager.

Firmness   To make the company's sales program and its objectives succeed, the sales manager must be firm in dealing with the sales staff and others. This is best accomplished through an open and understanding mind with access to facts that touch on all issues of any problem.

To maintain continuity, no salesperson should be treated above others in any manner, and discipline should be given privately, without theatrics, when necessary. No favoritism must be shown to any member of the sales force in making assignments, in providing company-owned property (car or other equipment), or in daily communications.

Insight   The sales manager acts as an information-clearing center for new ideas and information useful to sales goals. This includes receiving customer-initiated suggestions on current products, prices, competition, goals, and ideas. Salespeople develop intelligence on product improvements and developments, shipping methods, presentations, and other critical data.

Company advertising that solicits queries brings response (and thus new prospects to be given to territorial salespersons), while company management and employees funnel other opinions and viewpoints across the sales manager's desk.

With each new bit of knowledge, the sales manager reaches out to involve others (such as members of other departments, customers, employees, and salespeople) to determine the necessary information available for planning future goals.

Sense of Humor   As business and technological changes create more consumer goods that require sales, the sales manager faces ever increasing pressures to expand company markets, raise sales volume, lift profits, and all the while maintain a cool, relaxed, and detached viewpoint. The best weapon for such an approach is humor.

Humor, says John Jones, professor of communications at the University of Illinois, Chicago, is a valuable asset for those who hope to move into the executive suite. "Using humor in the office can create power," he says. "A person who is able to get co-workers to laugh has achieved a special sense of power because he or she is able to gain control over the group's sense of humor."

When the sales manager finds that humorous side in tense situations that demand immediate decisions and critical responses, he or she plants a strong foundation upon which the rest of the sales force can stand. In fact, says David Baum, a management humor consultant from Philadelphia, "appropriate use of humor in the workplace enhances communications, motivation, creativity, and ultimately production"—areas of special concern to the sales manager.

AREAS OF RESPONSIBILITY

To do the sales manager's job successfully, the former salesperson will have certain crucial areas of responsibility within which to determine future goals and objectives.

Planning

To ensure a continual flow of materials into a waiting market, the sales manager works with all corporate department heads to hammer out decisions on product choice, production, facility growth, financing, operations, employees, unions, community involvement, and other related efforts. Proposals must be based on accurate sales predictions and realistic expectations of company income in future years. Such information, formulated by the sales management area, considers a wide range of serious issues—economic conditions, resources available, industry growth, employee actions, markets available (current and projected), expansion into other markets, present and future competition, product evolution and acceptance—together with dozens of other vital needs brought together for long-range sales and marketing forecasts.

Organization

To implement the approved sales and marketing forecasts, the sales manager and staff separate all forecast areas into manageable territories. Salespersons and support staff are then assigned to individual territories to initiate fulfillment of the forecast. Like a highly trained football coach, the sales manager moves salespeople, supplies, product deliveries, and other needs where required. He or she is the final arbitrator of the problem attuned to obtaining the forecast results.

Direction

To ensure fulfillment of the forecast, the sales manager provides leadership, supervision, and direction of all those affected. He or she finds incentives and other rewards to provide motivation. Communication is maintained as necessary through a carefully established time-and-location operation.

Control

Acting as a control center, the sales manager matches forecast expectations with actual performance in the field (usually on a weekly basis). When serious contradictions and conflicts arise between the expectations and the forecast, it is the sales manager's responsibility to control activities and correct any problems that are discovered.

Recruitment

For the sales manager to be successful, as judged by sales volume, growth, and profitability, there must be a high-quality sales force at work.

Each company has its own sales expectations, methods, and goals. Generally, the larger the company, the more detailed those areas will be. Defining these specific areas by job analysis is the sales manager's first step in locating qualified salespeople. The job analysis details what specific knowledge (technical, business, financial, and social) is required, the type of customers targeted, territorial locations, anticipated travel costs, and necessary paperwork expected.

These efforts, which include the movement of people and equipment and the establishment of office and living quarters, require a detailed budget prepared by the organizing group and approved by company management.

With the job analysis completed, a full job description is assembled. This is finalized into a job specification listing that will include:

- job expectation
- education requirements and intelligence required
- relevance and importance of past experience and present experience required

- attitude
- health
- personality

The type of applicant needed is generalized in the job analysis, clarified in the job description, and fleshed out with details in the job specification. Often the more experienced sales manager does not need to prepare job sheets each time there is an opening in the sales force. He or she knows what type of person will best fit a specific position, and it is that person who is sought.

Recruitment can take place in many ways and from many sources. Examples are:

- within the company
- applications on file from past searches
- salespeoples' suggestions
- customers' suggestions
- hiring salespeople away from the competition
- trade-show inquiry responses
- employment agencies
- college placement offices and recruitment days
- newspaper and trade journal classified advertising

This recruitment effort provides the sales manager with a list of potential salespeople. With this list comes the process of applicant selection.

Choice To evaluate each applicant properly, the sales manager may establish the single interview method or create a two- or three-tiered interview system to narrow the original applicant list. The actual interview methods depend on company size, formality, sales force size and need, time allotted, and the need for new sales staff personnel.

The majority of company interviews require submission of a company-prepared application blank. These forms seek much of the same information provided by the applicant's resume—a reiteration of name, address, telephone number, personal information, past employment record, education, awards and honors, memberships, military history, and references.

The first interview of a three-tier interview is done through the personnel department to determine that all tangible requirements are met. The second interview can be directed by the sales manager's own office staff supervisor, who will seek to determine if the necessary intangibles are in place. The third interview, done by the sales manager, is a more informal meeting in which the personality, appearance, background, outlook, commitment, and future insights are observed in depth.

Whether loose and unstructured or formal and structured, the interviews are designed by the sales manager to reveal as much of the individual applicant's emotions, abilities, attitudes, and ideas as possible.

If the applicant passes the interview phases, he or she will most likely be required to take a detailed physical examination. This will determine the person's ability to perform on a job where physical endurance and stamina often are needed. A complete physical examination also will provide the company with all required information for its health care and insurance benefits programs.

In the same time frame, psychological tests will be given to determine the applicant's intelligence, honesty, sales attitude, character traits, personality, social influences, and other information needed to guide the sales manager's decisions.

Training   Every salesperson new to a company is not immediately sent on the road. It would be a foolish sales manager who would risk company customers, markets, reputation, and income by doing so. Most companies provide continuous training for their salespeople. These sessions include product information updating, sales methods, new operating procedures, advertising and promotional policies, in-house activities, incentive programs, and other specialized information that will be useful when in the field.

For the newcomer, more detailed sales presentations are given to orient that person to the company's purposes, goals, and methods. Such programs are twofold:

Formal and informal training.   At the corporate headquarters, the salespersons learn complete information on company products, history, personnel, policies and procedures, benefits, requirements, and other information. They learn how sales methods, principles, purposes, and goals blend into the big picture. This training is formal and presented in a challenging yet educational manner.

At branch offices the more informal sessions take place, with training that includes all local conditions, customer input, territorial review, and sales structure.

The more experienced sales staffers are often paired with the newcomer. They introduce the fledgling to customers, highlight the important aspects of dealing with others, and demonstrate how paperwork and other corporate-dictated policies are handled.

Enhancing employee morale.   The involvement in corporate and regional planning and operations is a boost for the newcomer. He or she acquires a sense of being part of the company family and an increased commitment reinforced by the training.

Additionally, customer relations with the salesperson and the company are improved through the added interest and attention the newcomer gives the customer.

Finally, such company efforts reduce the number of departures from the sales ranks while increasing profits based on the increased personal knowledge and ability of the new salesperson.

Direction

The sales manager, to be successful, must set an example by being a positive thinker. He or she must utilize motivational programs and speeches, incentive programs, and other opportunities for reward to bring about a higher success ratio.

Competition   Year-long incentive programs, contests with prearranged goals, and competition among members of the sales force provide a challenge that, when successful, brings out the best of each salesperson as well as increasing sales revenues.

Materials   The company product undergoes changes and improvements throughout the years. New competition arises. Economic trends develop and recede. Headlines highlight new international and national directions that influence company attitudes and actions.

The impact of such factors on the salespeople is resolved by a never ending informational supply sent from corporate headquarters to sales offices through the sales manager. Such information provides an effective communications flow that allows each salesperson to be as up-to-date as necessary for personal and company success.

The sales manager also makes the necessary telephone calls, business reports, and personal communications related to sales staff activities.

This company communication program reassures salespeople far from the parent company that they are not alone. Such material raises morale, creates a stronger sales effort, and establishes a strong working relationship between the sales manager and the sales force.

Evaluation

The sales manager must be able to efficiently and objectively provide top management with detailed evaluations of each salesperson. To do so dozens of individual information pieces must be assembled to show the salesperson's impact on company success or failure. Specific items to be measured can include the following:

- increase or decrease in goods sold
- effective communications between salesperson, sales manager, customers, and company
- delivery problems
- territory factors influencing sales
- customers lost or dropped or new customers found
- specific incidents during the year that influenced sales
- the salesperson's use of company information to increase and enhance sales and presentation

The sales manager must have the practical experience and knowledge from having been a salesperson to understand what happens in the territories he or she controls. Recognizing any problem that occurs, the manager can swiftly take action to maintain the forward-moving sales operation necessary for company success.

SACRIFICES

There is, however, another side to a manager's career that must be considered by those seeking management responsibility. It is a side that involves the sacrifice demanded for success.

The sales manager must sacrifice friendships. Once lifted from a sales force to head that group, the camaraderie must end. New rules, relationships, and responsibilities take over as the hard decisions affecting former peers can and sometimes do cause resentments. Tension, suspicion, and hostility can take the place of previous friendships.

The aware sales manager learns to deal with this loss through mental conditioning: the strengthening of that inner awareness of her or his own goals so that the feelings of others do not dictate her or his actions.

Sales managers sacrifice self-determination. A salesperson's primary responsibility centers around doing the sales job as he or she determines. As part of management, the individual accepts and promotes company policies and procedures, even if he or she disagrees with them.

Sales managers sacrifice a certain degree of compassion. Whether company-ordered or decided by the sales manager, the dismissal of a former co-worker can be painful on both sides. To do so swiftly and effectively the sales manager must give up the luxury of personal feelings. He or she cannot allow past good times shared to influence the decision.

The management team member quickly learns that equality, once so valued at the sales force level, does not truly exist throughout management. Indeed, the old line "it's lonely at the top" shows itself to be very true. Why? How?

In most organizations, even if there is a personnel flow chart predicting one's career for years ahead, this does not guarantee success. There will always be some who will seek the highest positions at any cost. The upcoming sales manager soon finds he or she must not only do an outstanding job each day but, while so doing, protect himself or herself from such corporate predators. A sense of wariness arises and unplanned, individual actions are carefully justified for self-serving reasons, while spontaneity and creativity fall away.

Soon those in management are perceived as apple-polishers who get ahead on gall rather than talent. The leaders who play this company game without alteration, regardless of how costly or destructive, can disrupt and destroy the most ambitious of those with management potential.

The rigid appraisal given by some corporate leaders of every area of an individual's life (clothing, cosmetics, family, office actions, personality), as if these must be exactly as prescribed by those on high, does a disservice to up-and-coming management. It is, however, a corporate fact of life.

Still, management is both the brain and heart of a company. From its brain, skilled men and women participate in the analytical oversight of the company's wide-flung daily operations. From its heart, department managers and line supervisors receive input from throughout the company's outposts, customers, competitors, and others. This information is analyzed, verified, evaluated, and passed on as necessary to the higher authority (the brain, or executive management) for action.

Today's management is in many ways the most educated, knowledgeable, informed, and creative leadership serving society. It is also the hardest-working, in on-the-job hours and in personal company/community relations. Management has learned through practical experience and trial-and-error methods not to accept simple solutions to complex problems. Instead, managers strive to find more effective methods and more attractive benefits for company, customer, and society, while working toward established goals.

Such management is strong in creative thought, able to develop innovative programs that reflect issues in multidimensional response, and capable of achieving desired results within specific time and budget limitations. It is this management form that will guide society's steps in years to come toward greater individual growth and stronger interpersonal relationships.

CHAPTER 5

WORKING WITH OTHERS

"Always do right. This will satisfy some people, and astonish the rest."

Mark Twain
To the Young People's Society

The new salesperson quickly learns the rudimentary techniques of selling in a day-to-day competitive atmosphere. The knowledge held and the skill by which it is applied lead to a greater awareness of personal success and failure.

In time, practical experience begins to take over the basic sales moves. The salesperson can be heard making comments like:

- "I already know what they need, but I still have to go through the motions."
- "I'll spend tomorrow stroking the customer's ego, but he (or she) will buy."
- "My product sells itself; I only write the orders."

Such comments may either highlight the salesperson's confidence in personal ability or reflect an attitude of taking for granted both product and customer. A problem arises when the customer recognizes this latter attitude through various shortcomings in the salesperson's efforts. These may begin with shortened telephone conversations or visits, quicker sales presentations with less visible enthusiasm, and failure by the salesperson to return or respond to customer calls and/or E-mail messages immediately. Worst of all, the customer finds less and less servicing of the salesperson's products, formerly done regularly and efficiently. In short, the salesperson is ignoring the customer's company needs.

The result is a dissatisfied customer given no choice but to seek new salespeople, those fresh and eager individuals *interested* in the customer's needs and willing to provide the necessary service. While this happens, the unknowing (or uncaring) salesperson goes about the motions of selling: indifferent presentations, a casual regard for customer viewpoints, and breaking of appointments until little credibility remains.

Customers recognize such attitudes more quickly than in the past and reject them just as quickly. They are far from the customers of earlier times, who simply accepted salespeople out of patience and courtesy. Today, salespeople are expected to be more oriented toward customer satisfaction than product distribution. This demands presentations and service that relate to customer needs, feelings, and goals.

INTERPERSONAL SKILLS

The salesperson who will succeed today recognizes that customers are more educated, more selective in their needs, and much more aware of available choices. This means that the salesperson cannot remain indifferent or disinterested in any customer and hope to accomplish company and personal goals.

Presentations must be given openly and honestly. Detailed and accurate information is mixed with the salesperson's outgoing personality to share company interests and customer preferences, recommendations, and needs. Such positive-oriented sales approaches remain the greatest sales challenge. Even when the information and materials that form the presentation become familiar and repetitive, today's salespeople employ many variations to hold customer enthusiasm and interest.

They also have discovered the necessary steps both within and outside their profession that help them work better and more efficiently with others. This in turn maintains their ever changing knowledge of what is and is not vital to personal career growth.

To work well with others, the salesperson must carefully prioritize relationships with those who influence her or his attitudes and career direction. The successful salesperson recognizes the many benefits that come from working with others, rather than in conflict with others.

Sales Manager

The sales manager, as the salesperson's immediate supervisor, is closest to the work situation. The sales manager is in a strong position to recognize the needs, goals, successes, failures, and the flaws within the salesperson, and to make needed positive recommendations for improvement.

He or she also can provide "hands-on" experience and advice as needed, take part in the salesperson's training programs, and point the way to additional materials to aid personal improvement and sustained career growth.

Peer Group

The salesperson is one face within the sales force. This group may work apart from one another (meeting only at specific times) or work within one office with daily contact. Though each sells the same product, based on the same materials and information, all presentations become individualized to specific customer interests.

Through comparison of personal sales techniques, insights, and understandings, salespeople enhance and enlarge one another's perspective within the sales force.

Company Management

As a direct company representative and a reason for its financial success or failure, the salesperson's duties are closely reviewed by all management levels. When necessary, the sales manager, under advice of executive management, will meet with the salesperson for evaluation, input, feedback, and any restructuring of the salesperson's programs and presentations needed to keep in line with company expectations.

Customers

The salesperson directs his or her knowledge, personal charm, interest, involvement, commitment, and other selling skills to the customer. The approval of the customer is positive proof that the many talents have been successfully brought into play. Yet if not for the comparable ability to deal effectively with receptionists, inner-office administrative assistants, and other office personnel, success might not be reached at all.

Competitors

In each selling opportunity, the salesperson is confronted with competition—sometimes seen, sometimes not. To present the company product successfully to critical and often demanding customers, the salesperson learns to learn, particularly to learn the competitor's product, value, quality, durability, and guarantees. This knowledge, mixed with equal amounts of self-confidence and company product quality, provides a lift to the aggressive and knowledge-based sales presentation.

This information, given through company management, department heads, specialists, and others, can be used to initiate needed changes within the sales area and maintain the enthusiasm already in place.

ACHIEVING PERSONAL GROWTH

Working around competitors on a daily basis teaches the salesperson what does or does not work. It allows her or him to work toward self-improvement in various areas.

Attitudes

Selling has been described as a lonely and often very painful occupation that does not allow the individual to reveal the true feelings within. Quite the contrary!

The salesperson, regardless of actual physical, emotional, or mental condition, must be on a constant social "high." The reason is simple: the salesperson must sell. To sell successfully, he or she cannot be totally open with anyone, as that "anyone" could well be someone who knows the customer's boss or secretary. This leaves neither time nor opening for the salesperson to be miserable, confused, or wracked with self-doubt.

It does leave time for paranoia—being fearful enough *not* to provide opinions or to reflect unsafe social viewpoints because someone may hear and tell. This rigid thinking, for an individual whose livelihood depends on establishing working relationships with all, is a serious problem at all sales levels. Often, it can lead to the concept proposed by Montesquieu: "I have ever held it as a maxim never to do that through another which it was possible for me to execute myself."

Such mental patterns call for a necessary, and valuable, self-assessment. In most cases, a better and stronger salesperson will emerge from such an evaluation—a person with thought-out attitudes required for successful selling. The beneficial traits formed will include the following:

- knowledge (having information available that is pertinent to the discussion)
- understanding (of the other person's viewpoint)
- patience (to accept opposite views without rancor)

Each of these traits will be reflected in an enthusiastic attitude of self-understanding, confidence, and sharing.

In the initial stages of personality development beyond paranoia and into self-assurance, such attitude changes may seem to some as contrived or forced. Yet in a short time this reevaluation and adaptation of self will change the salesperson into an individual able to effectively represent his or her company and deal firmly with those met in pursuit of sales orders.

This slow evolvement culminates with a primary value system beneath the wide umbrella called *integrity,* the consistency between what is said and what is done by the salesperson.

Integrity is the foundation upon which the salesperson constructs her or his career, social life, family, acquaintances, and all other facets of life. It is the difference to the customer between a product's reality and the customer's expectations of that product. If the salesperson promotes the product honestly and with confidence, and it performs as expected, the salesperson's integrity will be accepted. If the product exceeds the salesperson's assurances, and pleases the customer, then the credibility of the salesperson and the company rises. If the product fails after the salesperson's lavish presentation, customer trust and faith in that salesperson and her or his company will diminish.

Personality, Dress, and Grooming

The salesperson knows, first by company policy and then by practical experience, what her or his daily appearance is expected to be. He or she also learns the appropriateness of clean and well-pressed clothing, shined shoes, properly cut and cared-for hair, and well-maintained sales equipment and materials.

However, attractive clothing, aided by overall careful grooming, is not the only means to impress the company receptionists and inner-office administrative assistants and staff who work for the customer. The alert salesperson recognizes that the personality carrying the well-prepared image and materials will be an even greater asset when correctly presented to others.

In short, with a strong, positive personality aware of the visual and mental impact created, a salesperson does not enter a customer's work environment to slack off while waiting by smoking, littering, flirting with the office staff, or giving commands for immediate action. Instead, he or she is polite, sensitive, and businesslike in conduct (personality) and appearance (dress and grooming).

Sales Preparation and Presentation

Preparing and then presenting the sales material for highest impact allows the salesperson to learn company products and goals more thoroughly each time. It also provides an overview into the customer's needs relative to her or his company output and requirements. Each new piece of information made available to enhance the sales package is incorporated into the presentation material. The salesperson highlights these efforts through careful direction of the company's message toward the customer's basic interests.

STEPS TO SUCCESS

For the salesperson to succeed, to go as far and as high as possible, takes personal honesty and integrity, determination, and self-discipline toward that most critical part of the presentation—the salesperson's "self." We spoke earlier of the salesperson's attitudes, of a personal self-assessment which leads past paranoia into the outgoing personality and philosophy of successful selling. To reach that goal takes time, of course.

It takes critical evaluation and reorganization of one's life, attuned to the daily input of information gathered in such evaluation.

It takes an inner drive to recognize and then avoid those situations that can easily lead to following the view that says:

> "For of all sad words of tongue or pen / The saddest are
> these: 'it might have been'"

> —John G. Whittier
> *Maud Muller*

How does the salesperson go about making such a drastic changeover in life?

Self-Analysis

The salesperson begins self-evaluation by finding time to be alone, then listing, on one sheet of lined paper, her or his positive (good) points and negative (bad) points side-by-side. This is a free-association listing where anything in thought is written down.

Once the list is as detailed and complete as personal insights can provide, the salesperson puts each side into priority order. The best positive force starts the "good" side and the worst negative trait starts the "bad" side, until all habits are detailed in order of importance.

With a visual record of one's personal thinking about "self," comparisons are evident:

GOOD	BAD
warm and outgoing	easy to anger
intelligent	no general knowledge
practical	sometimes excessive

The next step is to ask opinions of peer group members, superiors, relatives, or any person who knows one's daily habits and attitudes. With those responses in hand (given as honestly and in as much detail as possible) the salesperson rearranges the original list to incorporate the views solicited. Reviewing the mixed list, it becomes easy to recognize that there is a middle ground between the good and bad points, a compromise from both sides toward another way that is more positive.

As the final list is developed, varied positions on each side can be incorporated into other views (for example, sharing can be placed with giving; indifference can fit under thoughtlessness).

Through this process, the salesperson soon will have perhaps ten or fifteen opposing attitudes, beliefs, habits, and reaction attitudes toward himself or herself.

Since the positives are counterbalanced by the negatives, this finalizing should highlight the compromise selection. In the above example, the list could now read:

GOOD	COMPROMISE	BAD
warm and outgoing	thoughtful	easy to anger
intelligent	well-read	no general knowledge
practical	reasonable	sometimes excessive

This compromise wording serves as a deliberate (and often-referred-to) guideline for the salesperson's dealings with others throughout the transition period and beyond. It isn't easy. Salespeople cannot wake up on Monday, proclaim themselves positive, and be that way by Friday.

It takes self-analysis, recognition, and acceptance of individual faults and negative qualities. Then through self-discipline and plain hard work, the salesperson removes the negatives, or changes them to positives.

Like the professional speaker who realizes he or she overuses "you know" in public speeches, there comes the realization that it takes a deliberate act of consciousness to resolve the problem discovered. Eventually, however, the problem *is* resolved.

Needs and Goals

A second effort of the salesperson is to prepare a detailed list of immediate and future *needs* and the *goals* that will require such needs. Although all salespeople are different in their needs, one primary area all must seriously consider is education.

As technology and communications change dramatically from day to day, the successful salesperson also will change to continually upgrade personal knowledge and skills. For the individual serious about such training, there is a wide variety of opportunities available.

In-House Training   All companies train their salespeople, first in the basics and then in the specifics, to meet customer needs.

Such programs can be informal talks between the new salesperson and the sales manager, classroom seminars and workshops held on a fixed time schedule, or accompanying a skilled salesperson making the rounds for a week or more. The emphasis of such training is to highlight what is involved in selling the company products, what is available to help that effort (market research and promotional materials), and what follow-up methods are utilized to bring the best results.

There is also the company library, where management has brought together books relevant to the company, its products, and its goals. There the learning-oriented salesperson will find specialized reports, product manuals (company and competition), industrial and manufacturing newsletters, trade magazines, and product-related newspapers.

Some companies encourage employees to become members of technical or professional societies or social organizations. These companies frequently contribute proper funds to cover any costs of participation.

Campus Learning   There are, scattered throughout America, many colleges and universities of all sizes that provide specialized training in any subject the salesperson might need.

Depending on the individual's sales position, obtaining a degree within her or his choice of fields may take longer than for the average college student, but the rewards—a stepping-stone to advancement, higher salaries, more opportunities, and greater recognition—make the effort worthwhile.

Often the company will offer a school tuition and expenses reimbursement plan to employees actively engaged in expanding educational horizons.

Correspondence Courses   If the sales position involves a large territory requiring many hours on the road each day, the salesperson has available to him or her varied specialized correspondence schools. Most of these courses provide workbooks, study guides, and cassette tape recordings dealing extensively with the subject matter. Though the salesperson has company presentations to review, reports to file, correspondence to complete, and orders to submit, correspondence courses do provide vital and necessary information. While on the road, the cassette recordings replace textbook reading to provide educational information of use to the salesperson when there are tests to be completed.

Though the learning salesperson has no direct access either to instructors or to school materials such as lab equipment, individuals skilled in the chosen study field are available for questions through telephone or on-line communications. There are also libraries in local communities that provide reference materials and other information as needed.

Workshops and Seminars   Outside the company there are hundreds of motivational and educational speakers and classes in areas vital to the salesperson's goals—from psychology to body language, from report writing to marketing techniques. For fees that range into the hundreds of dollars, the salesperson can spend one, two, three, or more days receiving intensive personalized training in her or his particular area of interest.

At the same time, such meetings provide the salesperson with the opportunity to talk and share with experts in the chosen field. Such networking is incorporated into the salesperson's daily activities as an enhancement of sales techniques and self-understanding.

Trade Shows   One of the most comprehensive industrywide learning opportunities is the trade show. Here the salesperson can find assembled almost every product created by the competition, complete with brochures, informational sheets, pamphlets, and live representatives (salespeople) to explain the products displayed.

This all-encompassing picture of the industry puts into perspective the salesperson's own place. It highlights the problems, purposes, and pursuits that lead to a successful career within the industry. It provides an opportunity for meeting new faces and sharing new ideas.

The trade show is the showcase of industry dedicated not to the salespeople involved, but to the individual customers whose ultimate decision toward such products will make or break any sales effort and salesperson.

Outside Influences

Although trade shows provide needed insights and information, the salesperson also has outside information sources to help him or her acquire additional knowledge and understanding of the market, customer, and product. These include the following:

Questionnaires Often part of company magazine and newspaper advertising, the returned questionnaire provides information revealing the potential customer's feelings and reactions toward the company product. Potential customers often give their name, address, and telephone number, thus becoming new prospects to the salesperson handling that particular geographical area.

Interviews On the street, in retail stores, at trade shows, and at special displays (state/county fairs, schools), a trained crew of company personnel conducts in-depth interviews concerning company products. Once this information is compiled and measured, it can serve as a realistic guide to all salespeople on customer expectations and beliefs.

Letters All companies receive mail from product users, either from the first level (purchasing agents or company buyers) or from retail customers. Some are filled with praise; others range from angry to disgruntled. These unsolicited views reveal customer reactions to products and seek immediate and personal attention by company representatives or the nearest salesperson. Through immediate response, the salesperson is able to reassure the customer while the letter is still fresh in mind and, at the same time, query as to what happened and why. The customer is continually reassured on the quality and dependability of the product in question and that the company will deliver on its product guarantee. If done properly and fairly ("Your letter helped us to see . . ."), the customer will feel justified in having written and more than willing to forgive error. If handled improperly, the customer will quickly look *not* for an immediate replacement of company product but for a new salesperson, while spreading the word of this problem to all available ears.

A benefit of such letters can be the indication of unexpected product defects. A salesperson should be concerned enough at such writings to initiate immediate steps to resolve the suspected problem.

SEEING THE FUTURE

As the salesperson expands her or his personal knowledge through education and experience, the possibilities for success open even further.

Promotion from salesperson to sales manager to department head to . . . the potential becomes mind-boggling.

To a young salesperson, such heavy dreams are not impossible. They do, however, require a detailed schedule of anticipated goals (to be completed by certain dates) and the order of accomplishments (with each completion leading to a higher, and more rewarding, position).

In larger company structures, the new employee finds her or his timetable for promotion already established. What would such a plan look like? From the company side, the salesperson's qualifications already indicate which promotional path will be followed. This information, culled from background, education, resume, application forms, interviews with references, and other sources, could lead to the following:

Name: Joshua Q. Morgan
Age: 22
Education: B.S.—Civil Engineering—2001
Present Position: Salesperson, Compressors
Hired: September 1, 2001
Background Work Experience: Three years part-time work
   with father's architectural firm and two years Engineer
   Two with Prosser Engineering, Inc.
Duties: Standard
Promotional Schedule (tentative)
   September 2001— Assigned salesperson, Portrero
      Section, Pittfield, Pennsylvania
   June 2004—Sales Manager, Regional Office, Chicago
      (initiate training program DELTA 4h3)
   October 2006—Manager, Design and Engineering,
      Regional Office, St. Louis
   January 2009—Creative Design Group Manager, St.
      Louis
   January 2012—Second Vice President, Engineering,
      Corporate Headquarters, New York
   January 2015—Vice President, Engineering, New York
   January 2018—President, New York
   January 2020—Chief Executive Officer and Chairman
      of the Board, New York
   January 2035—Retired

For the future company leader, however, there always will be the responsibility of acquiring the skills (such as management, administration, accounting, and technology) necessary for each upward step. Obviously the salesperson in this example will not be expected to practice good administrative and leadership qualities immediately, but he will be expected to do so at a future time.

From the time of hiring to each proposed promotion, the employee learns and improves *now*. If not, it is suddenly *later,* and there has been no reward because there has been no learning and growing into the more demanding positions.

To illustrate, on the above job promotion schedule, the initial engineering skills acquired at college will eventually be completely outmoded by new technology and techniques. The salesperson eager to succeed will recognize this problem and maintain a vigilance in personal education so that, as changes sweep through the field of knowledge, he or she can remain up-to-date and informed. At each step of a planned-out and prepared-for career, the individual must know where change will happen and how to accommodate that understanding into daily activities of advancement and growth.

As the salesperson expands knowledge, he or she becomes the product of careful planning, learning to handle customer objections and disagreements with poise, to present informative material as needed, to answer customer questions and concerns, and to commit to making the company's products satisfy the customer.

This style of honesty and openness is the salesperson's brightest moment, the sweet sense of success through self-pride and knowledge that removes the uncounted turndowns, such as:

"Nice presentation, but . . ."
"Nope, not interested . . ."
"Why don't you call back in a month or so . . ."
"Don't call us . . . we'll call you . . ."
"Maybe . . ."

For all the effort, time, patience, involvement, commitment, education, attitude, personality, hard work, self-discipline, and plain old determination, what does the salesperson receive in return? The following chapters will tell you.

CHAPTER 6

COMPENSATION

"The retail price of everything, what everything really
costs to the man who wants to acquire it, is the toil and
trouble of acquiring it."

Adam Smith
Wealth of Nations

Besides the emotional and mental satisfaction of doing the best
possible job, the salesperson is measured and rewarded for hard
work, knowledge, self-discipline, personality, enthusiasm, commitment, and achievement. In this, he or she receives a wide variety of tangible and intangible benefits.

Let's look more closely at a salesperson's total compensation
package. How are salespeople compensated? The answer is as varied as the sales positions available.

SALARY

Most entry-level sales representatives are compensated by salary
only during their training period. This provides them an income
while they learn their business (sales) and the internal machinery
of daily operations (the company).

There is, as we have shown earlier, much to learn.

What product or service does the company provide?
What is the sales territory and where is it located?
Who are the important customers?
Where are they located?

As the salesperson learns, the initial base salary is low (usually around $20,000) and there may be some commission or bonus available as additional incentive. Salespeople with college degrees in marketing or business administration receive a higher starting salary (high $20s or more) due to their knowledge and skill level in basic business operations.

In most entry-level positions, the salesperson is evaluated on anticipated long-term contributions. The initial salary, then, reflects the salesperson's potential value as perceived by the employer. The question under consideration is: Will the company receive full value for its investment in this new employee?

In addition to any salary provided is the employer's contribution of unseen costs available for the new employee:

health and life insurance
social security benefits paid at each payroll period
tuition payment for continued education
relocation expenses
recruitment fees

The corporation cost to provide these benefits and many more often will exceed 35 percent of the employee's base salary.

In the long run, a salary-only salesperson is at a disadvantage. Although it is secure to have a guaranteed salary, the opportunity to be paid for one's real worth is not possible. On salary, no matter how hard the salesperson may work, no matter how much travel is involved, no matter how many weekends are worked, the income remains unchanged. Eventually, the salesperson can, and will, lose personal motivation and enthusiasm. "Why work so hard to receive the same pay for less effort?" would be the oft-stated attitude.

Fortunately, most corporations recognize the need for enthusiastic representatives to sell their product. Therefore, they reward high-performance efforts with a commission and/or bonus program.

Many salespeople, if earning a straight salary base of $45,000 (with no commission), would perhaps become lazy and not perform to their full potential. Most personal needs are provided by the company through the high salary.

If salespersons know that their increased efforts for orders and increased sales production will enhance their comfortable living, they are going to work harder. If they know they also can increase income by moving into a commission basis, their motivation will become greater. Higher income will follow. The very real need for money is the strongest motive for salespeople to become successful.

COMMISSION

Once a true salesperson works on commission only and learns the satisfaction of being paid what he or she is worth, based on sales ability, it is very difficult to return to the salary-only status. He or she has learned that much higher income can be earned through the sales commission volume. That commission is a percentage of sales total determined by a variety of factors: territory size, customers served, previous performance, sales attitude, company goals and expectations, plus other factors contributing to sales success.

Often, commissioned salespeople will have a small base salary (usually $12,000 to $18,000). This ensures that he or she will be able to pay the bills from month to month, but it will not be sufficient to really put them into their personal financial comfort zone.

There are as many varied commission plans to compensate the sales force as there are companies to use them. The commission, as already indicated, can be a percentage of gross sales dollars (7 to 10 percent of the product price). This amount, when received, is credited to the salesperson's account, and he or she is paid on a regular basis from the account, as if on salary.

The major difference is the amount paid. It may vary upward or downward with each pay period, depending on the individual's abilities. Many times, these funds may be left in the account with only a designated amount withdrawn each pay period. This helps the salesperson set up the family budget and to know that, for the next several pay periods, he or she will receive that specified amount. Of course, should sales volume decrease, there will be time to increase sales efforts to maintain the established pay level.

One benefit of commission work is that, generally, the sales representative can earn a greater income than salaried people. Sales today is one of the highest paid professions in the United States. Many talented salespeople earn hundreds of thousands of dollars yearly, especially in the service industries (real estate, auto sales, insurance).

The insurance field is particularly noteworthy. Originally, most insurance salespeople came into the business kicking, screaming, and arguing. When they realized how much money could be made in the profession, their total philosophy changed. They had adopted Will Rogers's idea that "people's minds are changed by observations and not through argument."

They found, amidst the long hours, using evening and weekend time to meet potential customers, that the pay was high due to annuities (continued commissions) paid, as each sold insurance policy was renewed.

The sales representative, in the first year, builds a careful base of solid customers. As these customers' policies are renewed, the salesperson continues to be paid a monthly commission. After the second year, he or she earns added income on policies sold the first year, along with commissions sold on newer policies. It is very common for a five-year insurance salesperson to earn $50–$60,000 yearly while the amount continues to increase with each new year.

Even when the sales representative leaves the company or assumes a position with another firm, the funds keep rolling in. Salespeople who have successfully built their careers over ten years of continued service within the industry often earn $200,000 yearly—and more.

In the product area, there are cases of "super salespeople" who earn more than $10,000,000 in commissions! Keep in mind, however, the price these people pay in terms of hard work, travel from home, and maintaining that maximum effort nonstop simply to achieve such an income level.

Such success can be accomplished through strong and challenging goals, hard work, and the drive to excel.

Many successful salespeople may not seem overly smart in person, but in action they work harder, put in more effort, have more smarts, and don't quit until they accomplish their goal: an order taken from a satisfied customer.

Median Annual Earnings of Various Sales Personnel

According to the U.S. Bureau of Labor Statistics, as reported in the 2000–2001 *Occupational Outlook Handbook,* the following are 1998 median annual earnings of various sales personnel:

Sales Representatives (except retail) $36,540, including commission. The lowest 10 percent earned less than $19,220 and the highest 10 percent earned more than $83,000 a year.

Median annual earnings in the industries employing the largest number of sales representatives, except for retail, were:

electrical goods $36,700
paper and paper products   36,700
machinery, equipment, and supplies   36,400
professional and commercial equipment   35,300
groceries and related products   31,900

Services Sales Representatives (in selected business services, including commission) $34,910. The lowest 10 percent earned less than $17,640 and the highest 10 percent earned more than $79,790 a year.

Median annual earnings in the service industries employing the largest numbers of sales agents in selected business services were:

computer and data processing services $41,200
management and public relations   34,000
mailing, reproduction, and stenographic services   33,100
miscellaneous business services   29,500
personnel supply services   28,500

Services sales representatives are paid under various systems. Some receive a straight salary; others are paid solely on a commission basis—a percentage of the dollar value of their sales. Most firms use a combination of salary and commissions.

Advertising Sales Agents (including commission) $31,850. The lowest 10 percent earned less than $16,210 and the highest 10 percent earned more than $83,080 a year.

Telemarketers and Other Related Workers (including commission) $17,090. The lowest 10 percent earned less than $12,350 and the highest 10 percent earned more than $30,290 a year.

Sales Engineers (including commission) $54,600. The lowest 10 percent earned less than $30,560 and the highest 10 percent earned more than $97,700 a year.

Median annual earnings in the industries employing the largest number of sales engineers were:

computer and data processing services	$62,800
electrical goods	56,600
professional and commercial equipment	51,700
machinery, equipment, and supplies	48,900

Securities, Commodities, and Financial Services Sales Representatives $48,090. The lowest 10 percent earned less than $22,660, and the top 10 percent earned more than $124,800.

Median annual earnings in the industries employing the largest number of securities and financial services sales representatives were:

securities brokers and dealers	$53,700
security and commodity services	46,900
mortgage bankers and brokers	36,300
commercial banks	33,000

Financial services sales representatives usually are paid a salary; some receive a bonus if they meet certain established goals. Earnings of financial planners can be wholly fee-based, which means they do not receive any commissions for selling a product they recommend. They simply charge by the hour or by the complexity of the financial plan. The majority of financial planners, though, receive commissions on the sale of insurance products or securities, in addition to charging a fee.

Insurance Sales Workers $34,370. The lowest 10 percent had earnings of $17,870 or less, and the top 10 percent earned more than $91,890.

Median annual earnings in the industries employing the largest number of insurance sales workers were:

fire, marine, and casualty insurance	$34,100
insurance agents, brokers, and services	33,200
medical service and health insurance	31,600
life insurance	31,500

Many independent agents are paid by commission only, whereas sales workers who are employees of an agency or an insurance carrier may be paid in one of three ways: salary only, salary plus commission, or salary plus bonus. In general, commissions are the most common form of compensation, especially for experienced agents. The amount of commission depends on the type and amount of insurance sold and whether the transaction is a new policy or a renewal.

Real Estate Agents (including commission) $28,020. The lowest 10 percent earned less than $13,800 and the highest 10 percent earned more than $83,330 a year.

Median annual earnings in the industries employing the largest number of salaried real estate agents were:

residential building construction	$32,300
real estate agents and managers	25,500
real estate operators and lessors	19,100

Real Estate Brokers (including commission) $45,640. The middle 50 percent earned between $28,680 and $80,070 a year.

Commissions on sales are the main source of earnings of real estate agents and brokers. The rate of commission varies according to agent and broker agreement, the type of property, and its value. The percentage paid on the sale of farm and commercial properties or unimproved land is usually higher than the percentage paid for selling a home.

Retail Sales Positions Earn the federal minimum wage, which was $5.15 an hour in 1999. In areas where employers have difficulty attracting and retaining workers, wages tend to be higher than the established minimum.

Median hourly earnings of retail salespersons, including commission, in 1998 were $7.61. The lowest 10 percent earned less than $5.76 and the highest 10 percent earned more than $14.53 an hour.

Median hourly earnings in the industries employing the largest number of retail salespersons were:

new and used car dealers	$15.10
department stores	6.90
miscellaneous shopping goods stores	6.70
family clothing stores	6.40
women's clothing stores	6.20

Compensation systems vary by type of establishment and merchandise sold. Salespersons receive hourly wages, commissions, or a combination of wages and commissions. Under a commission system, salespersons receive a percentage of the sales that they make.

Marketing and Sales Worker Supervisors (including commission) $29,570. The lowest 10 percent earned less than $16,700, and the highest 10 percent earned more than $71,910 a year.

Median annual earnings in the industries employing the largest number of salaried marketing and sales workers were:

new and used car dealers	$50,100
grocery stores	24,900
miscellaneous shopping goods stores	22,400
department stores	21,900
gasoline service stations	21,000

Compensation systems vary by type of establishment and merchandise sold. Many managers receive a commission or a combination of salary and commission. Under a commission system, retail managers receive a percentage of department or store sales. These systems offer managers the opportunity to significantly increase their earnings, but they may find that their earnings depend both on their ability to sell their product and on the condition of the economy. Managers who sell large amounts of merchandise often receive bonuses or other awards.

Travel Agents (overall and in the passenger transportation arrangement industry, where most work) $23,010. The bottom 10 percent of travel agents earned less than $13,770, and the top 10 percent earned more than $34,670.

Salaried agents usually enjoy standard benefits that self-employed agents must provide for themselves. Among agencies, those focusing on corporate sales pay higher salaries and provide more extensive benefits, on average, than those focusing on leisure sales. When they travel for personal reasons, agents usually get reduced rates for transportation and accommodations. In addition, agents sometimes take "familiarization" trips, at no cost to themselves, to learn about various vacation sites. These benefits attract many people to this occupation.

Earnings of travel agents who own their agencies depend mainly on commissions from airlines and other carriers, cruise lines, tour operators, and lodging places. Commissions for domestic travel arrangements, cruises, hotels, sightseeing tours, and car rentals are about 7 to 10 percent of the total sale, and for international travel, about 10 percent. Travel agents also may charge clients a service fee for the time and expense involved in planning a trip.

During the first year of business or while awaiting corporation approval, self-employed travel agents often have low earnings. Their income usually is limited to commissions from hotels, cruises, and tour operators and to nominal fees for making complicated arrangements. Established agents may have lower earnings during economic downturns.

INCENTIVES

Salespeople, even the best, get lazy. How, then, can companies motivate them to achieve their potential?

Many corporations set performance goals and, to those who achieve those goals, provide cash bonuses, merchandise, gift certificates, vacations, and other material goods designed to increase sales and profits.

One entire industry serves companies promoting ideas and awards. It is the incentive business, comprised of companies selling packaged goods (travel programs, merchandise, and awards programs). This industry sponsors representatives who put together individual sales contest programs for particular clients.

Most sales contests provided in this manner are geared to achieve specific sales goals within a set time frame (usually a three-month period, or one quarter of the fiscal year). The sales representatives who achieve over 100 percent of quota for the specific period chosen usually will receive an expensive and often glamorous prize. Depending on the corporation, prizes could range from a steak dinner at a fine restaurant to a Hawaiian trip for two.

Many companies have yearly and quarterly contests to provide continual motivation for top performance attitudes from all salespeople. This offers many benefits, including providing the salesperson who has no wins in the first quarter the opportunity to win during the next three quarters or to win in a variety of other competitions available.

BONUSES

It is traditional that each employee receive some type of bonus at year's end. It may be a token of appreciation for a well-done job or a major cash or gift award.

Many bonus programs are designed so that participants know through weekly or monthly feedback their standing against all others—a spur to greater participation and sales dedication. This also allows for constant "tweaking" of the almost-made-it salesperson's efforts to maintain performance geared to winning the major prize or cash award.

Bonus opportunities can be quite lucrative in the sales profession, especially when geared to a percentage of all sales over 100 percent of quota. For example, one major corporation begins to pay bonus premiums when the salesperson reaches 90 percent of quota, and continues to pay up to 150 percent of quota for the year. They will pay several hundred dollars per point, or percentage, over quota. To the salesperson who achieves 124 percent of quota, the program bonus could reach 35 percent of total sales. A sales representative who earns $40,000 under such a program would also receive $14,000 as a bonus.

The discretionary bonus, rather than that paid on sales performance, may or may not be paid. This type of bonus is paid only at the discretion of the company's sales manager. Set amounts to be awarded are established, and sales representatives may wind up being paid more or less, dependent on how well they are liked by management, whether they had a good year, and other nonquantitative criteria. This type of bonus encourages playing up to the boss and is really more of a nonincentive to perform well. It is not unheard of that a top sales producer will receive a small discretionary bonus simply because he or she had problems with the boss.

NONCASH INCENTIVES

A study of any detailed compensation survey conducted by major periodicals will show that, among top management, salaries comprise only a small percentage of total income. For example, the chief executive officer of a large transportation company receives an $800,000 salary plus deferred income and stock options worth an additional $2,500,000. Why, he or she might rightly ask, receive a large salary, when the Internal Revenue Service will seek to take most of it away?

The smart executive will almost always defer most income and, in so doing, maintain control of it. Such insight is expressed well in the television commercial that says: "It's not what you make— it's what you keep that counts!"

Most salespeople do not have to worry about deferred income. They do, however, take advantage of some unique noncash benefits (often referred to as "perks and lurks"). These can include both tangibles and intangibles.

Company Automobiles

Most firms provide an automobile for use by the salesperson as both company and personal car. All expenses incurred, plus insurance and associated costs, are paid by the company.

Expense Accounts

These can be unlimited and serve to entertain clients and management as needed. Many companies provide an account for key salespeople to use when clients come to town. Others advance money to cover incurred expenses and ask the salesperson for an accounting via the dreaded "expense report."

Some salespeople can become very creative when preparing expense reports. They will turn in receipts for meals not eaten, miles not driven, and other fraudulent expenses. Fortunately, most of these individuals are discovered and find new opportunities and time to be equally creative while in the unemployment line.

Low- or No-Interest Loans

Loans at little or no interest are often corporately provided to aid employees in times of financial need, for vacations, or for a large-item purchase.

Educational Assistance

Many firms provide reimbursement for books, tuition, and travel costs for those attending college or seeking advanced degrees in specialized fields. It is done within the company's continued-learning programs.

Insurance and Other Benefits

Life, health, and dental insurance, prescription drugs, and/or eyeglasses may be provided at little or no cost. Additionally, some employers have in-company medical assistance (checkup, prescriptions, immediate nursing, advice, classes toward health improvement), day care centers (for working mothers and fathers), parking areas, and indoor/outdoor recreation areas.

Relocation Expenses

All moving costs between company facilities may be paid, plus meals and living accommodations while waiting for the new home to be ready.

Vacation Time and Sick Leave

Vacation is a special part of each person's work career. Depending on length of service and job requirements, companies now will provide continual paychecks (straight salary and/or average commission income) for the vacationing or ill employee.

There are many other intangible benefits available to employees. Each company establishes specific policies regarding these benefits, and the wise employee soon learns these policies.

The most intangible perk, however, is the one most overlooked in the sales profession. It is unique to salespeople and cannot be seen, touched, or smelled. It is the set of individual skills developed by the employee while working for the company.

Salespeople, as part of their job, learn the product and distribution system of the company, who the customers are, and what they will purchase. These salespeople have become, through this increased knowledge, more marketable to new employers. This translates into higher income, greater promotional opportunities for management-oriented individuals, and the chance for a richer and fuller lifestyle.

Sales is one of the few professions today to offer this wide diversification of opportunities in combination with a freedom to set one's own working schedule to fit the individual's pace and style. Such independence, when carefully managed, provides a freedom that few other positions can enjoy. Others are instead relegated to an office routine that rarely varies. These workers become content to work each day as an echo of the last. To a salesperson, such routine would be unbearable.

Part of the joy of selling is never knowing for sure what will happen next. What objections will a buyer suddenly have? What event will change the selling situation? Who will be met and shared with today? It is this uncertainty that stimulates and challenges the salesperson to success.

Those who will be successful in sales thrive in such an environment. They will not become bored with their jobs. If things should become stale and routine, they know their skills are marketable. They will quickly turn toward another opportunity that will return to them the excitement and challenge once held. At the same time they will earn a higher income without the drawbacks they may currently be experiencing.

Most salespeople are strong in character and not afraid to hear the word "no," even at high volume from a potential buyer. "No" to these salespeople means they are one step closer to selling the product or service, for in that single word they hear a challenge to their personal selling skills. By providing them an objection to overcome, the buyer gives information and responses the salesperson needs to sell that customer.

The salesperson who is put off by a "no" or any negative comment about her or his product, service, or presentation will surely fail. "No!" is what sales is all about!

To turn "No!" into "Well, perhaps . . ." and ultimately into "Yes!" is the ability of the true salesperson who enjoys the challenge of give-and-take and who, through personal ability and knowledge, consistently earns substantial income to put the finer things into her or his life.

CHAPTER 7

SALES OPPORTUNITIES IN MANUFACTURING INDUSTRIES

"Everything is sweetened by risk."

Alexander Smith
Dreamthorp—On the Writing of Essays

Sales careers are many and varied. All salespeople must, in the beginning days of career planning, determine in which direction they wish to grow. All sales careers involve the need to motivate a prospective buyer to purchase the offered product of a company salesperson.

For a product to be sold, it must first be designed and manufactured, tested and approved by the company and any required state and/or federal agencies, packaged, advertised, and then effectively distributed into the selling channels.

Because only one or two of every ten new products succeed in the marketplace, careful planning is vital to a business hoping to capture a projected market share. The first necessity for the sales force is to define the product's strengths and weaknesses, the markets in which the product will compete, and the target sales goals.

STRATEGIC PLANS

A good strategic plan includes long-range goals, objectives for the product, and dealing with future improved versions. This plan will be founded on a strong market orientation that is based on the viewpoint of the ultimate customer. This sample product profile will include the following:

- compatibility with current product lines
- appeal to current customers
- number of potential customers
- market size and growth trends
- seasonality
- degree and nature of the competition
- price structure and competitive advantage
- service requirements

Priorities of a typical manufacturing firm in evaluating new product potential will be as follows:

- Do we have the marketing/sales skills needed?
- Can we obtain patent protection?
- Does the product match our manufacturing capabilities?
- Is the market large enough?
- Are the unique product benefits communicable and believable?
- Can we make a profit?

A manufacturing concern seeks new customers, in addition to current customers, in an extended-market penetration or a product line extension. To obtain this goal, one typical method is to introduce a "new and improved" item every eighteen months. This is accomplished by following four important manufacturing rules that often lead to the success of a product or product line.

- Manufacture a quality product that provides a good value as perceived by the customer.
- Provide technical competence throughout the management and sales forces.
- Develop the technical skills and sales ability of the sales and company representatives.
- Constantly evaluate progress made in the field during the product introduction phase to determine what changes are needed within the program.

CUSTOMER COMMITMENTS

Once the product has been designed and manufactured, it is the sales department's responsibility to obtain initial customer commitments. New markets must be identified, and a game plan must be developed to capture maximum market share. The resultant sales plan is basically a strategy to determine distribution channels through defining the middleman structure and establishing incen tive packages needed to get first-time purchases from new and existing customers.

Prepurchase and postpurchase services are usually the first and second reasons given for industrial market sales. Products usually rate third. An example of service before the sale is the industrial distributor who meets the customer, studies the need, gives alternatives, and prepares the design for the manufacturer's product installation. This distributor makes money on the product sale but, without the service beforehand, there could be no sale. Within the industrial market, the need for service after the sale is obvious and is a major reason for repurchasing the product.

It is, however, the salesperson who must actually take the new or existing product into the field and obtain orders. A salesperson working directly for a manufacturer is usually assigned a specific geographical territory. This can range in size from one part of a large city to the land mass of several states. Within this assigned territory are key account customers who make up a significant portion of the salesperson's customer base in terms of business volume. Such accounts tend to be major regional retailers or national chain stores that sell to consumer and industrial users. Other territory accounts are smaller retailers, distributors, and product users. They purchase less than key accounts and almost always at higher prices.

There may be only a few accounts, or literally thousands of customers, serviced by one salesperson. It is that individual's responsibility to visit each potential customer, present the features and benefits of the company's new products, learn the needs and goals of each customer, and finally write the first of many orders.

At the retail level, salespeople sell products to everyday consumers. These products may include home computers, VCRs, clothing, giftware, automobiles, food, health and beauty aids—anything that may be purchased in a store. Everyone who enters a retail store is a customer with the potential to buy. More importantly, each such individual can be turned into a repeat customer through effective sales techniques.

Many retail salespeople are compensated by a small base salary plus a commission (a determined percentage of sales income paid by customers). The more a retail salesperson can persuade the customer to purchase, the higher her or his commission will be on the sale.

Some sales representatives, such as those working for automobile dealers, are a paid straight commission only on each car sold. They live and die daily to achieve their assigned sales quotas and to earn maximum commission and bonus dollars.

In a retail environment, such as a large department store, sales help receives a base salary and sometimes a small commission. Their purpose is not to "hard sell" customers but to assist them by means of recommendations, personal attention, and available information; thus the phrase: "May I help you?"

This phrase offers the salesperson's knowledge and experience to the customer. In so doing, it effectively camouflages its true purpose: to close the sale so as to gain additional profit margin for the store while providing the best available service for the customer's benefit.

ADVANCEMENT

Retail sales careers lead, in many cases, into sales force management, store management, and into management of varied business segments (such as men's shirts, ladies' purses, or dinnerware). Those with talent and dedication often find themselves promoted to run an entire operation, either within a single outlet or a multi-store chain. At this point, the salesperson becomes management. He or she is responsible for hiring, training, and motivating the sales force toward achievement of corporate objectives. Many times this is educational, rewarding, and growth-oriented for the individual. Success seems likely and, in our American culture today, it is often described as "rising to the top." In the case of the sales representative being promoted into sales management (see Chapter 4) such a step also can become a disaster.

Good sales representatives do not always make strong managers. They are used to achieving set goals and enjoying the praise and monetary benefits of their individual accomplishments. When promoted into management, they no longer have that personal responsibility for their individual sales performance levels. They do suddenly have sales quotas to set for their sales force, programs to administer, and individuals to motivate and inspire daily to achieve required sales levels.

The transformation from superstar salesperson to sales manager can be devastating, unless the salesperson can intensify self-discipline and organization dramatically. To do so indicates the ability to adapt and assume responsibility necessary for such management.

As a salesperson, the representative could set her or his own schedule as determined by sales territory priorities. A manager must have not only a nine-to-five regime (at least), but also the skills necessary to motivate the sales force to reach top performance levels and, in so doing, earn more financial security and benefits than sales management may make.

As a rule, managers do earn more than sales representatives, but not always. A high-quality sales representative working on commission can easily earn several times more than her or his manager. This is because the sales representative is compensated for her or his own performance only, on a pay plan that rewards quota achievement. As an example, M. Smith sells computer products to industrial users. He is paid a base salary of $24,000 and can earn a 10 percent commission on all products sold within his territory. During the past year, Smith sold $4,500,000, and in so doing, earned a commission of $45,000 over and above his base salary. He was also given a bonus of $10,000 because he produced more than his quota, which was $3,750,000.

In our example, our sales representative, Smith, was paid a total of $24,000 salary, plus $45,000 in commissions, plus a $10,000 bonus, for a total income of $79,000. His manager, however, was paid a base salary of $55,000, but earned no commission because she does not directly sell to customers. She did earn a bonus of $12,000 because her sales force achieved the quota set by senior management, for a total income of $67,000. This is not a bad salary, but it is lower than that of the star salesperson.

Sales representatives in the wholesale product area, whether industrial or consumer-oriented, do not sell to the general public. Their customers' needs are oriented toward other corporations, which will either use their product internally or sell it to users. In such a position, the sales representative must be an expert on all company matters, from product specifications to corporate policy. He or she must handle buyers who seek special favors (longer credit terms, special advertising funds to promote the product to potential customers, and the like).

When selling a consumer-oriented product, such as coffee makers, the sales representative (company employee) will most often work closely with independent manufacture representative firms, referred to as "manufacturer reps." These rep firms receive a commission by the product manufacturer for any product sales within an assigned geographical territory. A salesperson working for the manufacturer would be responsible for several rep firms within her or his assigned region or territory. The rep firm employs several sales representatives of its own. Its job is to be as close to potential customers as possible. These reps introduce new products, policies, and sales personnel from the factory to potential and current buyers. It is these reps who must establish and maintain good relationships with product buyers. Good sales representatives understand the market forces in effect within the territory, internal and external, and any impact they have on current and future sales programs.

The manufacturer's salesperson works closely with an independent representative, who is also paid by the same manufacturer. The difference is that the salesperson has responsibility for the performance of the rep firm but may or may not have ultimate authority, based on experience, to hire or fire the rep firm. It is the salesperson's responsibility to monitor the performance of the rep firm in each product category and, by customer accounts, to determine if maximum coverage is being provided by the rep. Since most salespeople will earn commissions based only on sales performance, it is in their best interest to have high-quality, motivated, and knowledgeable sales rep firms working for them in the territory. This means frequent trips in the territory with the rep firm's salespeople to meet customers and ensure the highest level of sales volume.

Manufacturers, in addition to selling to retailers, often sell to distributors first. The distributors then establish a retail distribution network, comprised of many small retailers. The distributors buy manufacturers' products at a lower price than the small retailers would pay if they bought directly from the manufacturer. This is because the distributor buys a much higher quantity, and thus qualifies for lower pricing. Also the distributor handles the extra paperwork, servicing, and phone calls generated by the many small retail outlets. The distributor also performs valuable services to the retailer (such as inventory monitoring, retail sales force training, and advertising design for special promotion events) that the manufacturer could not provide to so many small retailers. The cost would be too high for such a level of service from a manufacturer but not for a distributor.

Since the distributor is buying for several small retailers, the distributor is able to pool orders to obtain the best pricing. This enables distributors to be competitive in the marketplace they service. The savings are passed on to retail customers, who now can offer savings to the ultimate customer, the consumer.

Whether the salesperson works for a large or small retailer, distributor, or product manufacturer, he or she carries the direct responsibility for identifying new customers and meeting sales objectives. Without the sales representatives' consistent effort and perseverance in their duties, products from all sources could not, and would not, be brought to market as efficiently and quickly as they are now.

CHAPTER 8

SALES OPPORTUNITIES IN SERVICE INDUSTRIES

"The greatest thing a human soul ever does in this world is
to *see* something, and tell what it *saw* in a plain way."

John Ruskin
Modern Painters (1856)

It seems that every day our society is becoming more and more
service oriented. This is reflected in the greater variety of services
now being offered to corporations and individuals. At one time,
the potential salesperson who desired to enter the sales field, in either industrial or consumer products, found a limited market in
which to operate. Now the field is much broader due to a tremendous growth in new service industries.

There are two areas to explore when considering a service industry career: well-established companies in proven fields or
emerging growth-oriented industries.

The companies that provide services to corporate customers and
individual consumers must have a sales force able to sell a product
that cannot be touched, tasted, worn, and sometimes not even used
(such as life insurance). The salespeople employed by such firms
must be able to sell an intangible product. This is always a more

difficult sale to achieve. On the positive side, most services have a built-in repeat customer factor. If the salesperson has instilled a sense of customer satisfaction, he or she may enjoy the benefits of additional business due to customer loyalty. For example, the travel agent who planned your first vacation to a once-in-a-lifetime destination made sure your airplane seats were located near the front of the plane because he or she took time to find out your preferences. Your hotel room was an upgrade suite at no extra charge, and the complimentary theater tickets were an added bonus. Are you likely to use a different travel agent to plan and arrange your next business trip or vacation?

There are so many services offered by corporations that salespeople, whether entry-level or experienced, need only target the type of service they would like to sell.

There are two basic types of services: those sold to other corporations and those sold directly to consumers. There are always new, emerging service companies in both sectors with innovative products (services) either to better satisfy a need or create a need where none existed.

SERVICES OFFERED TO CORPORATE USERS

A few of the services sold to corporations are described in the following pages:

Advertising

Every day we are aware of the magnitude, power, and high visibility of advertising. Opportunities for sales representatives include selling in radio, television, magazines, newspapers, direct mail advertising, and advertising agencies. There are thousands of radio stations, advertising agencies, and newspapers and magazines that require the selling ability of skilled salespeople.

Beginning a career in this field is a strong step toward successful career development.

It is true that "advertising sells" but not until a salesperson sells the advertising concept. The salesperson brings together, as a package, the talents of art directors, artists, filmmakers, market research directors, print production managers, and photographers in order to solve the problems of her or his potential clients. Salespeople who sell advertising time or production services must know how the services they offer will best present the products or services of their clients to their customers.

Many sales representatives begin their advertising careers in smaller agencies or at production houses (companies that produce actual print or photographic materials) because of the opportunities for learning and advancement. Working for a smaller firm provides exposure to more agency functions than working in a more well-known company.

Radio and Television

The selling of radio and television time, not to be confused with the sale of advertising materials, is one of the more glamorous sales positions. Many new salespeople are attracted to this industry because of its excitement. It is, however, a challenging and rewarding career area, even beyond the evident glamour. Most salespeople in this field are paid on a commission-only basis. They sell air time to corporate clients, either manufacturers of products or producers of services. Many sales are made to advertising agencies who buy air time for their clients.

This type of intangible sales does have advantages. The value of advertising has been documented time and again. Why else would a corporate sponsor spend more than $300,000 for a thirty-second television spot (not including actual costs to produce the commercial)?

There is a great deal of income to be made in selling advertising time to corporate clients, and competition is keen for available advertising dollars. Salespeople in this field are well-organized, very aggressive, enthusiastic, and always knowledgeable about those services they sell.

Telecommunications

With the breakup of the world's most efficient and highest-quality telephone system, opportunities to provide top-quality telephone voice and data communication services are expanding. Almost all corporations make use of long-distance telephone calls to contact customers, outside sales representatives, and vendors and suppliers. With the sudden cost increase of long-distance service, many companies have begun selling less-expensive, yet high-quality, telephone services.

Selling long-distance voice services is only the tip of the telecommunications iceberg. Other areas include data communications via modem (one computer "talking" with another via telephone lines), teletext (written messages transmitted to video terminals), and video conferences (executives at diverse locations "meeting" via two-way television hook-up).

Another service capturing market share is the fax (facsimile) machine, a machine about the size of a copier that transmits and receives documents and photographs quickly via telephone lines to locations anywhere in the world. This machine has changed the way companies do business through a fast and economical transmission of documents. In fact, this is an example of service as product. The fax machine is sold as a service (quick document transmission). The buyer, however, actually purchases, or leases, a machine (product). Leasing is a possibility, but continued cost reductions of fax machines induce most corporations to purchase rather than lease. The customer buys the product to obtain the service offered.

It is interesting to note that fax machine manufacturers are competing not only against their competitors but against those companies that provide next-day courier services. Such companies have now found themselves in intense competition. The reason is that the cost of sending an overnight letter via next-day mail has skyrocketed. A fax letter sent anywhere in the United States will cost only as much as a quick long-distance phone call, and it will be received instantly!

TRAVEL INDUSTRY

Within this multifaceted industry there are many career opportunities for the aggressive salesperson. Airlines, cruise ship companies, hotels and motels, travel agencies, and corporate meeting planners all provide services to their corporate clients. Executives of corporations would prefer to delegate the responsibility for planning business trips and incentive travel to others. Such an individual is a specialist in corporate travel planning. This salesperson makes all travel and hotel arrangements, plans sightseeing trips for groups when required, and often travels with the client to be sure everything is right.

Other salespeople are assigned responsibility to promote incentive travel to corporations as a sales incentive for sales force members. For example, if a corporate salesperson attains quota, he or she could win an expense-paid trip for two to Hawaii. It is the salesperson who must sell the corporate decision maker on the contest's value to employee and to company.

The travel industry is large and well established. Those who seriously consider a career in this field should spend time at their local library reviewing the hundreds of books devoted exclusively to this business.

COMPUTER INDUSTRY

This industry has seen tremendous growth during the last decade. In the early days, anyone able to sell could easily land a position as a salesperson in the hardware or software industry. Because very few people could understand what made computers work, most people were afraid of the machines, and it was a time of rapid technological advances.

Today, however, salespeople must be fully versed in what computers can do for the customers. Most computer-service companies sell either programming abilities or computer use (large-frame machines that are both powerful and expensive). Companies with neither expertise nor capital to purchase these machines still have need for computer-processing time. Computer company salespeople sell time on the computer. For example, a company may need to process its payroll each week but cannot afford a computer. By buying computer time from a payroll service company, they can now process their payroll inexpensively.

As with the travel industry, the computer services business is tremendous in scope. There are more varied opportunities than could be listed in several volumes (sales of timeshare, custom and prepackaged software, computer program development, computer system design and development, and applications). The industry today changes so fast that even experts have a hard time keeping up with the new technology.

CONSULTING SERVICES

Many salespeople today provide services to companies on how they might operate more efficiently. Consultants specialize in every field: accounting, computers, product design, packaging, how to sell products and services, and training and development programs. Those salespeople who sell consulting services need to first understand the problem the customer has before they can sell the solution.

The salesperson may represent a large consulting firm or be an independent and self-employed consultant. In either case, the buyer purchases expertise to resolve problems within the corporation and looks to the salesperson for solutions.

Most consultants have a wide variety of resources from which to select the correct mix of services for the client. These can include communications, marketing, internal training programs, personnel development, real estate, office space design and layout, and product design.

The successful consulting salesperson is a creative problem solver with a real desire to help others. Often he or she obtains "hero" status with clients by finding solutions to problems the company could not resolve on its own. Also, a good consultant salesperson is a good teacher with the ability to show others how to accomplish their goals and objectives.

SERVICES SOLD TO CONSUMERS

What about intangible sales to the individual consumer? There are many examples.

Insurance

Salespeople may work for either an insurance company or for an independent insurance agency.

Salespeople who work for an insurance company sell only that company's products. A salesperson at an agency selling many insurance companies' products sells varied products depending on which company has the best products for her or his customer.

There is a tremendous amount of money to be made in the insurance industry. Salespeople are paid a commission during the policy life of those they sell. The longer they remain in sales, the more policies they sell. Incomes of more than $100,000 in this business are not unusual.

Financial Planning

Financial planning is a real growth industry. Most consumers are in poor financial shape, have no real budget, and often owe too much to credit card companies at exorbitant interest rates. Financial planners sell a service of complete family financial planning and investment. They make recommendations as to what insurance is best or what investment vehicle will pay for the children's college education.

Many times a financial planner can make the difference between a family's surviving and managing its own financial affairs or being forced into bankruptcy.

Financial planners often work for a division of a large corporation, such as a major insurance company. They are not insurance agents, however. They are able to sell insurance plus other investment vehicles that insurance agents cannot sell.

There are numerous examples of how a salesperson can sell an intangible service to corporate or consumer customers. The rewards are usually higher in terms of added compensation, flexible hours, and advancement opportunities. New services are constantly being developed that produce even more opportunity for the aggressive salesperson.

Sales representatives sell a service and in doing so give themselves the best in terms of career development, income, and lifestyle. They have made the commitment to be the best in a highly competitive environment, and to enjoy the daily thrill of knowing that this type of selling, though not for everyone, has given them the best life has to offer.

SALES AND MARKETING PROFESSIONAL ASSOCIATIONS

American Marketing Association
  311 South Wacker Drive, Suite 5800
  Chicago, IL 60606
  E-mail: info@ama.org
  www.ama.org

American Society of Travel Agents
  1101 King Street
  Alexandria, VA 22314
  www.astanet.com/

Association of Retail Travel Agents
  2692 Richmond Road, Suite 202
  Lexington, KY 40509
  www.artaonline.com/

The Certified Financial Planner Board of Standards
  1700 Broadway, Suite 2100
  Denver, CO 80290-2101
  www.cfp-board.org

Direct Marketing Association
  1120 Avenue of the Americas
  New York, NY 10036-6700
  www.the-dma.org/

Manufacturers' Agents National Association
P.O. Box 3467
Laguna Hills, CA 92654-3467
www.manaonline.org

Manufacturers' Representatives Educational Research
Foundation
P.O. Box 247
Geneva, IL 60134
www.mrerf.org

Marketing Research Association
1344 Silas Deane Highway, Suite 306
Rocky Hill, CT 06067-0230
E-mail: email@mra-net.org
www.mra-net.org/

National Association of Insurance and Financial Advisors
2901 Telestar Court
Falls Church, VA 22042-1205
www.naifa.org/

National Association of Realtors
777 Fourteenth Street NW
Washington, DC 20005
E-mail: InfoCentral@realtors.org
http://nar.realtor.com/

National Association of Sales Professionals (NASP)
8300 North Hayden Road, Suite 207
Scottsdale, AZ 85258
www.nasp.com/

National Retail Federation
325 Seventh Street NW, Suite 1100
Washington, DC 20004
www.nrf.com/

Sales and Marketing Executives International
P.O. Box 1390
Sumas, WA 98295-1390
E-mail: smei@earthlink.net
www.smei.org/

Sales and Marketing Management International
Statier Office Tower
Cleveland OH, 44115

Sales Professional Network
http://cbpa.louisville.edu/salesnetwork/

The Securities Industry Association
120 Broadway
New York, NY 10271
www.sia.com

APPENDIX B

SALES AND MARKETING PUBLICATIONS

Advertising Age
www.adage.com/

Managed Care: an on-line magazine for the managed care executives with news links and articles that could assist sales efforts in the managed care areas.
www.managedcaremag.com/

Pharmaceutical Representative: a monthly news magazine dedicated to pharmaceutical sales professionals, managers, and trainers.
www.pharmrep.com/

Sales and Marketing Management
www.salesandmarketing.com

The following are publications from the American Marketing Association:

Journal of International Marketing
Journal of Marketing
Journal of Marketing Research
Journal of Public Policy & Marketing

Marketing Educator
Marketing Health Services
Marketing Management
Marketing Research

The following are publications of the Marketing Research Association:

Alert!
Blue Book
Connector

The following are publications of the Direct Marketing Association:

The DMA's State of the Interactive E-Commerce Marketing Industry Report: 2000
Washington Report

JOB-LOCATING RESOURCES

The American Marketing Association
Career Center
www.ama.org/jobs/

Direct Marketing Association
Job Bank
www.the-dma.org/jobbank/

Jobs: Sales and Marketing
www.jobsjobsjobs.com/category/marketing.html

MarketingJobs.com
www.marketingjobs.com/

Marketing Research Association
Classifieds
www.mra-net.org/docs/resources/classifieds.cfm

Medical Sales Associates
http://msajobs.com/index.htm

National Association of Sales Professionals
Career Opportunities
www.nasp.com/SalesJobs/careerframe.html

Sales Career Network
   http://cbpa.louisville.edu/salesnetwork/career.htm

Sales and Marketing Careers
   http://votech.about.com/education/votech/msubmenusales.htm

Team Marketing Report
   (For sports marketing positions)
   www.teammarketing.com/jobopps.htm

TRAINING PROGRAMS FOR SALES AND SALES-RELATED CAREERS

You will find most sales-training programs in community colleges. Do an Internet search for sales courses in the geographic region that interests you, and you'll be surprised at the number of hits you will get.

There are also many institutions nationwide that offer courses in sales-related fields, such as marketing, advertising, public relations, journalism, communications, and others. Check the Internet and college guides at your local library.

In addition, several professional associations offer training programs. Here are three examples. Your own search will no doubt reveal more.

Marketing Research Association
www.mra-net.org/docs/products_services/training.cfm

Sales Education Network
http://cbpa.louisville.edu/salesnetwork/education.htm

Sales and Marketing Training Programs
http://votech.about.com/education/votech/cs/
educationsales/index.htm